American Gangster

John Dillinger and Al Capone - 2 Books in 1

Roger Harrington

Copyright © 2017.

All rights reserved. No part of this publication may be reproduced, distributed, or transmitted in any form or by any means, including photocopying, recording, or other electronic or mechanical methods, without the prior written permission of the publisher, except in the case of brief quotations embodied in critical reviews and certain other noncommercial uses permitted by copyright law.

This book is intended for informational and entertainment purposes only. The publisher limits all liability arising from this work to the fullest extent of the law.

Table of Contents

John Dillinger

Introduction

Early Life

Jail Time

First Robberies

Lima Jail Break and Dillinger Gang Robberies

Crown Point Jail Break and the second Dillinger Gang

Lincoln Court Shootout

Little Bohemia Lodge

Public Enemy #1

Plastic Surgery

The Last Days of the Dillinger Gang

Betrayal and Death

Conclusion

Al Capone

Humble Beginnings

Early Career

Moving On

Gaining Influence
Centre of Attention
Victims and Events
The Quest for Justice
Final Days
The Capone Legacy

John Dillinger

Public Enemy: America's Most Notorious Gangsters

Roger Harrington

Introduction

In the period following World War 1, America enjoyed a period of extreme prosperity. The "Roaring Twenties" saw a boost in industry and production, as well as a new, more relaxed lifestyle. Americans indulged in hot jazz music, illegal speakeasies, and reckless spending.

The prosperity led to stock market speculation. Speculation means that people were buying stocks for products they assumed would increase in value due to the widespread prosperity and overproduction. It also meant that people were buying and selling arbitrary stocks while they were very valuable, regardless of history of the company, or what the stock represented. It was an economic bubble. Banks were also doling out easy credit to many individuals looking for more money to back the artificially inflated stocks.

The economic boom meant that farms and industries were able to wildly over-produce their products. However, as is explained by the rule of supply and demand, too many of the same product on the market means that each individual product is devalued.

America could not go on giving credit to people who bought over-inflated stocks for companies that were over-producing their products. The bubble had to burst. London's stock market crashed on September 20th, 1929, leading to a panic in America. Stocks were shaky, and the economy was on the verge of tanking. Despite numerous attempts to inject capital into stocks to save the economy, as was done during the 1907 crisis, the market still fluctuated uneasily. Individuals and companies alike began to sell their stock at a rapid rate.

On "Black Monday", October 28th, 1929, the DOW fell by 38.33 points, or 13%, as a selling panic began. On October 29th, 1929, now famously known as "Black Tuesday", a record number of stocks were traded, and the DOW fell by an additional 30 points, or 12%.

Thus began the Great Depression. Investment in American industry dropped dramatically, leading to a decline in the once-booming industry. This, in turn, lead to unemployment as plants and factories had to be shut down; leading further to a marked lack of spending by the American people. It is estimated that as many as 15 million Americans were out of work at this time.

Banks were closing with great speed and taking customers' money with them. Nearly half of America's banks were forced to close during the crisis. Many citizens were without jobs or steady incomes. It was one of the worst economic climates in American history. The us/them mentality was stronger than ever as common people turned against the remaining banks, considering them to be heartless institutions that stole money from loyal customers while the American people suffered en masse.

Outlaws like Bonnie and Clyde, and "Pretty Boy" Floyd became heroes in the eyes of the American people. These people rolled up to banks and demanded money; a feat that many destitute Americans dreamed they could do. The robbers were considered Robin Hood type characters; giving the evil, rich banks what they deserved after treating their customers so poorly. However, these thieves weren't stealing from the rich to give to the poor, as Robin Hood did; they were stealing from the rich to line their own pockets.

Nevertheless, as newspapers continued to report on the exploits of the outlaws they became celebrities in their own right; as recognizable and idolized as any movie star. It was the perfect environment for the handsome, charming, and cunning John Dillinger to round up a gang of robbers and take the American banks by storm.

Early Life

John Herbert Dillinger was born on June 22, 1903 in Indianapolis, Indiana. His mother, Mary Ellen Lancaster, died of a stroke when John was only three years old. His father, John Wilson Dillinger, owned a small grocery store in the city. John Sr. was a religious man, who reportedly alternated between abusing and spoiling his son; beating him, then giving him money for treats, or locking him in the house, then allowing him to stay out all night.

After his mother died, John was largely raised by his older sister, Audrey and her husband until their father remarried in 1912. There are rumors, though unsubstantiated, that John hated his stepmother at first, but the two eventually grew closer and began a three-year sexual relationship.

John's teenage years were filled with fights, various petty crimes, and all night parties. He even had a childhood gang he dubbed The Dirty Dozen who terrorized younger children, vandalized, and stole. He earned the nickname Jackrabbit for how spry he was, and how nimbly he evaded the police.

John quit school at the age of 16 and began working in a machine shop. Though he was a good worker, he continued his hard-partying lifestyle. John still liked staying out all night and committing crime.

John Sr. grew tired of his son's misdemeanors, and worried about his future. He decided to sell his grocery store and move the family to a small town, in the hopes that getting away from the corrupting influence of the big city would help his son settle down and stay out of trouble. In 1921 the Dillingers moved to Mooresville, Indiana.

John Sr. did not get his wish. His son continued to commit petty crimes and live his wild lifestyle. Soon after the family moved, John was arrested for auto theft. He then made his first of what would be many escapes from police custody. Knowing the police were after him and that he could not return home, John Dillinger enlisted in the U.S Navy.

Dillinger made it through basic training and was posted on the now-famous U.S.S Utah, the ship that was sunk during the 1941 Pearl Harbor attacks. Dillinger was not exactly a regimented rule follower. He resented the strict, by-the-book lifestyle he was supposed to lead and, when the ship was docked in Boston, Dillinger deserted, only 5 months after he enlisted. John was eventually dishonorably discharged from the U.S Navy.

Dillinger made his way back to Mooresville in 1924, where he met and married 16-year-old Beryl Hovious. The couple, being young and unemployed, moved in with Dillinger's father. John just couldn't stay away from the criminal lifestyle. He was once arrested for stealing chickens. John Sr. was able to smooth things over with the owner and the matter was settled out of court. The already strained father-son relationship got worse.

John and Beryl then moved to her parents' home in Martinsville, Indiana. John got a job in an upholstery shop, and began playing shortstop on the neighborhood baseball team. On the field he met Ed Singleton, another petty criminal, and a distant relative of his stepmother's. Singleton was Dillinger's first partner in crime. The two men began a robbery plot.

Singleton knew of a grocer who would be carrying his weekly receipts on him after work. He said John could easily rob the man, while Singleton worked as the getaway driver. John carried a .32 caliber pistol, and a large metal bolt wrapped in a handkerchief.

The plan was to hit the grocer over the head with the bolt, knock him out, and take his money. Instead, when John struck the grocer, the man put up a fight and, in the ensuing chaos, the pistol accidentally discharged.

John then assumed he had shot the man, and ran to find Singleton. Some accounts say that the two men attempted the robbery together, were recognized by a local pastor, and turned in to the police. Some say John attempted to robbery alone, and when he went to take his getaway car, Singleton was nowhere to be found, leaving John to wander the streets and eventually be picked up on suspicion by the local cops.

Regardless, Dillinger and Singleton were eventually caught by police and brought before a judge. Although Singleton had a previous criminal record, he was also equipped with competent legal counsel. The man pleaded not guilty and received a sentence of two years in jail. Singleton would later die after passing out drunk on a railroad track.

The prosecutor told John Sr. that if his son were to plead guilty, he would receive a lenient sentence. Dillinger went in front of the judge without a lawyer. Assuming he would just receive a slap on the wrist he took his father's advice to plead guilty. However, he didn't receive the leniency he was told to expect. In a surprising turn of events, John Dillinger was convicted of assault and battery with intent to rob, and received a sentence of 10 to 20 years of jail time, to be served in the Indiana State Reformatory.

This was a truly shocking sentence for a comparatively paltry crime. Embittered with the prospect of facing so many years in prison, John was quoted as saying, "I will be the meanest bastard you ever saw when I get out of here."

Jail Time

Dillinger was incarcerated in Indiana State Reformatory in 1924. He played on the prison baseball team, and was a model worker at the prison's shirt factory. Accounts say he routinely finished his own quota quickly, and worked to fulfill the quotas of his fellow workers. This, and his charming personality, made him popular among other inmates.

He was, however, far from a model prisoner. Dillinger tried to escape several times, and befriended many hardened criminals who began to educate him on the ins and outs of robbing banks. For Dillinger, the old idea that prison is just criminal school was beyond true. The legend of John Dillinger began in prison. He would never have reached such a celebrity status without the knowledge he gained and the men he met in Indiana State Reformatory.

At first Dillinger's wife, Beryl Hovious, wrote and visited him frequently. After a while, though, she became weary of the distance between her and her husband. She was still very young, and facing the possibility of up to twenty years without her husband weighed heavily on her. She began visiting and writing less frequently, and eventually filed for divorce on June 20th, 1929, just two days before John's 26th birthday. Dillinger was devastated. Soon after this crushing event, he was denied parole. John was to stay in prison to at least serve the minimum time he was given. Dillinger became even more despondent.

He asked to be transferred to Indiana State Prison, from the Indiana State Reformatory. The Prison was stricter on inmates and much more regimented. Prison officials were unsure why a man who had so much trouble with authority would ask to be moved to a harsher environment. When asked, John claimed the prison had a better baseball team. Still suspicious of his motives, but not willing to pass up an opportunity to give Dillinger a stricter environment, officials approved the transfer.

Dillinger didn't end up joining the prison baseball team. Instead, he teamed up with his friends from the reformatory, Harry

Pierpont, and Homer Van Meter, who had been transferred a few months prior. Career criminals with no intention of letting prison reform them, the men were already planning a jailbreak, and several bank robberies for when they got out of jail.

Dillinger and his crew also met Walter Dietrich, a man who had worked with one of the most notorious bank robbers of the time, Herman Lamm. Dietrich taught the men the meticulous methods used by Lamm to pull off successful heists. Lamm was known for doing detailed research before hitting a bank. He knew the bank layout, the location of all the valuables, the movements of the guards and workers, and where the nearest police station was.

Pierpont and Van Meter had the knowledge and the plans in place, but they still needed to actually get out of jail to go ahead with their perfectly-crafted robberies. To do that they would need a man on the outside to outfit them with guns, and money to bankroll the escape. John had a significantly smaller sentence than his friends and would be getting out much earlier. Pierpont and Van Meter brought Dillinger on to aid them in their escape. They informed Dillinger of reliable accomplices and safe houses, and gave him a list of banks and stores that would be good bets to rob.

The plan was fast-tracked in May of 1933 when Dillinger's stepmother fell ill. He was released on parole on May 10th, 1933 after serving only nine and a half years of his ten to twenty year sentence. His stepmother died before he arrived home, but at least John was free.

First Robberies

John Dillinger was released from prison at the height of The Great Depression. With no legitimate job prospects to fall back on, and his friends in prison relying on him for escape, he immediately turned to crime again. Just six weeks after his release he committed his first bank robbery to begin to get the money necessary to break his friends out of jail.

On June 21st, 1933, Dillinger and two unidentified men (most likely members of Pierpont's gang) robbed the New Carlisle Bank in New Carlisle, Ohio. The men made off with $10,800. The Dayton Daily News reported that the bandits snuck into the bank at some point during the night, and ambushed the first person to arrive to work that morning, clerk Horace Grisso. Dillinger and his crew bound any bank staff that entered the building while they were waiting for access to the vault.

Dillinger and his accomplices continued in this way; using Herman Lamm's meticulous bank robbing techniques to pull off well-crafted heists.

On July 17th, 1933, Dillinger robbed The Commercial Bank in Daleville, Indiana, making off with $3,500. A few weeks later, on August 4th, he stole $6,400 from the Montpelier National Bank, also in Indiana. Just ten days after that heist he robbed the Bluffton Bank in Ohio of $6,000. Police began tracking Dillinger from that point forward.

He had a distinctive bank robbing style, often displaying his athletic prowess by vaulting smoothly over teller counters.

On September 6th, 1933, Dillinger robbed one last bank to ensure he could carry out the plan. At the Massachusetts Avenue State Bank in Indianapolis, Indiana Dillinger made off with $21,000. He now had sufficient funds to bankroll the prison break. Though his friend Homer Van Meter, who had originally planned the escape, had actually been paroled on May 19th, 1933, the plan was still to go forward, ensuring Pierpont and his gang was made free men.

On September 22nd Dillinger was arrested in connection with the Bluffton robbery after the police received a tip about his whereabouts from the landlady of an old girlfriend John had recently visited. He was sent to a prison in Lima, Ohio to await trial on the charges. While being searched at the prison, guards found a mysterious paper among Dillinger's belongings. It looked like plans for a jailbreak, but Dillinger refused to explain the paper's significance.

Four days later, on September 26th, 1933, ten men Dillinger met in Indiana State Prison used the jailbreak plan to escape. Dillinger had used the money from the bank heists to buy weapons and bribe key figures at the prison. He smuggled seven .45 caliber pistols into the prison in a barrel of thread meant for the on-site shirt factory.

Harry Pierpont and Russell Clark told the shirt factory superintendent, George Stevens, he was needed in the basement. There he was jumped by the rest of the gang and taken hostage. Walter Dietrich went and found deputy superintendent Albert E. Evans and claimed he needed the man's help to break up a fight in the factory basement. Evans was also jumped by the gang and became their second hostage.

Pierpont had been harshly disciplined by Evans during his stay at the prison. He used this opportunity to get revenge on the man who had terrorized him for months. Dietrich actually had to stop Pierpont from going too far and severely hurting, or killing Evans; more because it would put a kink in their plan than because he had any respect for Evans' life.

Foreman Dudley Triplett happened to be heading to the basement for supplies and, though he was not part of the original plan, was also taken hostage. Luckily for the criminals, their gang was large enough to deal with the need to take surprise hostages.

The men made Stevens lead the way through the prison. They concealed their guns under stacks of shirts and slowly made their way through the prison. The rest of the guards and prisoners didn't seem to notice what was going on.

There were four gates standing between the men and their freedom. At the first gate

Stevens was forced to tell the guard, Frank Swanson, to let the party through, or they would kill him. Swanson became yet another hostage. The gang got through the second gate in the same way, with more threats of violent death. At the third gate they used a metal shaft from the factory as a battering ram, and burst open the door themselves.

Guard Fred Wellnitz was badly beaten until another guard, Guy Burklow, opened the outer gate of the prison. The men and their hostages were now in the lobby of the prison's administration building. The gang herded the eight prison workers they found there into the prison's vaults. Joe Burns shot 72-year-old Finley Carson twice for not moving fast enough.

At that moment, the warden, Louis E. Kunkel, came into the lobby. He was made to join the rest of the workers in the vaults. The gang then walked out the front door of the prison.

Harry Pierpont, Charles Makley, Russell Clark, Ed Shouse, John Hamilton, Walter Dietrich, James Clark, Joseph Fox, Joe Burns, and Jim Jenkins were now free men.

Dietrich, James Clark, Fox, and Burns went one way. They immediately ran into Sheriff Charles Neel who had just performed a prisoner intake in the administration building. The men overpowered him, stole his weapons, and took him hostage. They forced him to drive them away from the prison. They abandoned the sheriff's car near

Wheeler, Indiana, and stole another vehicle, which quickly blew a tire. The men were now on foot, and lost in a dense, wet forest.

Eventually the group began to see their hostage, Sheriff Neel, as a burden. They fought over what to do with him. James Clark was also becoming troublesome to the rest of the group, complaining of stomach problems. Neel and Clark split from the group. Clark released Neel in Gary, Indiana, and the lawman immediately had Clark arrested and sent right back to prison.

Pierpont, Russell Clark, Ed Shouse, John Hamilton, Charles Makley, and Jim Jenkins all went another direction when they escaped the prison. They had help from the outside and went to gang accomplice Mary

Kinder's house. She had agreed to help the men find safe houses and evade the law if they would include her brother, Earl Northern, in the escape plan. Northern, however, was in the infirmary at the time of the escape and had to be abandoned.

Kinder still followed through on her promise to help the men, and set them up with new clothes, and a hideout in Hamilton, Ohio. Most of the men in Pierpont's group would soon join Dillinger and come to be known as The Dillinger Gang. Unfortunately for Jenkins, while on the way to their safe house in Hamilton, the men had to evade the police. During a chase the car door swung open and Jenkins fell out. The rest of the men couldn't risk going back for him. He was killed that night.

Pierpont, Shouse, Clark, Hamilton and Makley got safely to Ohio where they used the hideout in Hamilton, as well as Pierpont's parent's house, to plan yet another jail break.

Lima Jail Break and Dillinger Gang Robberies

Now that Dillinger's friends were out of prison, they planned to return the favor, and spring John from the Lima jail.

On October 12th, 1933, Harry Pierpont, Charles Makley, and Russell Clark, all recent escapees from Indiana State Prison thanks to Dillinger, embarked on a mission to free their friend from where he was being held in Lima, Ohio.

Sheriff Jess Sarber and his family lived in a house on the same grounds as the jail. He, along with his wife and Deputy Wilbur Sharp, had just finished dinner, and had moved to the Sheriff's office to talk. Pierpont,

Makley and Clark came to the office claiming to be police officers needing to transfer Dillinger back to Indiana State Prison in connection with outstanding charges at his previous place of incarceration.

Sheriff Sarber, asked the men for credentials that would corroborate their story. Pierpont then fired his gun twice, hitting the sheriff once. The men took the keys to Dillinger's cell, and locked the deputy and the sheriff's wife in the basement to ensure a quick and uninterrupted escape. Sheriff Sarber died of his wounds about two hours after he was shot.

Dillinger, Pierpont, Makley, and Clark fled to Chicago to meet up with the rest of the gang. They plunged headfirst into a life of crime. Realizing they would need much more firepower to pull off the robberies they had planned, the gang decided to raid a police arsenal for supplies.

They used the same detail-oriented approach they used in bank robbing when they cased the arsenal. It turned out the stash was poorly guarded and would be easily taken over by Dillinger and his crew. They raided the arsenal and made off with multiple guns, a load of ammo, and bullet proof vests.

The men then embarked on a spree of bank robberies. They hit the Home Banking Company in Saint Mary's, Ohio for $12,000. A few weeks later they stole $74,802 from the Central National Bank & Trust Company in

Greencastle, Indiana. Just a month later they hit the American Bank & Trust Company in Racine, Wisconsin, making off with $28,000.

By this point the gang was infamous. The way they went about their business in an almost gentlemanly manner gained them great popularity among the American people.

The gang always wore suits and fedoras to their robberies, and was generally gracious to the bank's customers and workers. No drug or alcohol use was permitted during the planning or carrying out of any robbery, leaving no room for error. The men split the loot evenly and planned heists meticulously. They were consummate professionals, often keeping business hours when planning and executing their robberies, then going home to their families just like legitimate businessmen.

John Dillinger's name was even used to sell cars in ads that claimed Dillinger would never be caught if he continued to drive a Ford.

Chicago police were becoming increasingly agitated by both the existence of The Dillinger Gang, and their growing popularity. On December 14th, 1933, Detective William Shanley was following up on a tip that the Dillinger Squad may have been responsible for a robbery committed the previous day. Shanley approached John Hamilton at a garage where he was having his car detailed. Hamilton shot and killed Shanley, then escaped.

Chicago police set up a taskforce made up of as many as 40 men, led by Melvin Purvis. They were called The Dillinger Squad, and their one task was to find The Dillinger Gang and bring them to justice for their robberies and the murder of Detective Shanley.

Things started going south for the gang on January 15th of 1934. While Makley, Pierpont, and Clark were lying low in Tucson, Arizona, Dillinger and Hamilton planned a heist of the First National Bank in East Chicago, Indiana. During the robbery, Dillinger got into an altercation with Officer William Patrick O'Malley and ended up shooting him eight times in the chest, killing him. The men still managed to steal $20,000, but Dillinger was now wanted for murder.

Dillinger and Hamilton journeyed to Tucson to meet back up with the rest of the gang. They were staying at the Hotel Congress when a fire broke out on January 21st, 1934. All guests were forced to evacuate the hotel. Some members of the gang had to be rescued through a window, and down a fire truck ladder.

They were not permitted to bring their luggage but, as the gang had guns and money in their bags, they did not want to leave the luggage to burn up in a fire. Makley and Clark tipped firemen $12 each to go back and get their valuable luggage. Among them was William Benedict

A few days later, Benedict was reading a copy of True Detective, a true crime magazine, and recognized the men who asked him to retrieve their luggage. He told police the gang had been in town. Tracing the luggage firemen had pulled from the building, police found Makley's bags at a gang safe house, 927 North Second Avenue. On January 25th police went to the residence and took Clark into custody.

Makley was followed by police and arrested at the Grabbe Electric and Radio store where he was attempting to buy a radio that would pick up police frequencies. Pierpont was caught in a staged traffic stop, lured to the police station, and arrested. Dillinger was also taken into custody at the same safe house police found Clark. All together the police found $25,000 in cash and several stolen guns on the captured gang members.

A debate ensued between all the states where the men were wanted criminals. Since the gang had hit banks in Ohio, Indiana, and Wisconsin, all three states wanted to extradite the men and bring them to justice in their state.

Pierpont, Makley, and Clark were sent to Ohio to stand trial for Sheriff Sarber's murder.

Ed Shouse, one of the escapees from Indiana State Prison, and ex-member of the Dillinger gang, testified against Pierpont, Makley, and Clark. His testimony helped rack up charges against the gang members. In the end, both

Pierpont and Mackley were sentenced to death, and Clark was given life in prison.

On September 22nd, 1934 Pierpont and Makley attempted yet another jailbreak. Makley was shot dead in the escape attempt. Pierpont was wounded, but survived, and was executed as planned on October 17th. Clark spent much of the rest of his life in prison. He was released on medical parole in 1968, but only survived a few months out of prison. He died of cancer on Christmas Eve, 1968.

Crown Point Jail Break and the second Dillinger Gang

Dillinger was extradited to Crown Point, Indiana where he was supposed to stand trial for Officer O'Malley's death. He was placed in the Crown Point jail that local police deemed "escape-proof". The sheriff held a press conference outside the jail where she and several important members of local law enforcement were photographed palling around with Dillinger.

There are differing accounts of what happened next, but one thing is certain, Dillinger proved the jail was definitely not escape-proof.

One account says Dillinger's crooked lawyer managed to smuggle a gun into John's cell, which he then used to break out. Another account says he fashioned a wooden gun out of a shelf in his cell. Yet another account claims Dillinger carved a gun out of either a bar of soap, or a potato, and blackened it with boot polish.

Whether the gun was real or not, the guards on duty on March 3rd, 1934, believed it was. Dillinger and another prisoner, Herbert Youngblood, escaped from Crown Point jail with a guard as a hostage. Security around the prison had been relaxed from where it was when Dillinger first arrived, and the men were able to walk the streets unseen and unbothered.

Dillinger and Youngblood took the guard to a local garage where they took a worker as another hostage, and stole a car that belonged to the county sheriff.

It was then that John Dillinger made a mistake that would ultimately lead to his downfall. He drove the stolen car across the Indiana-Illinois state border, violating the National Motor Vehicle Theft Act. The Bureau of Investigation, a precursor to the FBI, could now be involved in the manhunt for Dillinger. It seems odd, with so many robberies, jailbreaks, and even a murder under Dillinger's belt, that this would be the crime that would involve national law enforcement, but it was technically his first federal offense.

J. Edgar Hoover, the director of the Bureau of Investigation, jumped at the chance to hunt down Dillinger. Hoover hated Dillinger's popularity, and the fact that crime was being celebrated in America. Hoover went on to use many of the facts from the Dillinger Gang and other Depression-era outlaws to get the creation of the Federal Bureau of Investigation approved.

Although local and national law enforcement agencies were on the hunt for Dillinger, his biggest problem after escaping from the Crown Point jail was that his faithful gang members, Pierpont, Makley, and Clark were all in prison. Dillinger needed a new gang.

Some reports say that Lester "Baby Face Nelson" Gillis actually helped Dillinger escape from Crown Point in exchange for Dillinger's membership in Nelson's gang. Others say that Dillinger went to his old Indiana State Prison friend Homer Van Meter looking for men to outfit a new gang. Regardless of how it began, two of the most notorious bank robbers of the 1930s were now working together.

The Second Dillinger Gang (as some news outfits dubbed it due to Dillinger's popularity) consisted of Dillinger, Nelson, Van Meter, John Hamilton, Tommy Carroll, and Eddie Green. This gang was a far cry from the calculated and meticulous First Dillinger Gang. Nelson was known as a hothead who enjoyed getting into fights, and enjoyed firing his gun.

The first robberies committed by the new gang did not go as smoothly as earlier robberies. On March 6th, 1934 the men hit Securities National Bank & Trust in Sioux Falls, South Dakota. All the gang members were doing their jobs: Carroll was on lookout outside the bank, Hamilton sat in the car ready for a getaway, Dillinger, Van Meter, Green and Nelson all entered the bank to perform their assigned duties.

Of Nelson, Tommy Carroll was quoted as saying, "That guy would walk into hell and back on a job. He's a mental case otherwise, but he would fight the devil when we were hitting a bank". He proved that to be true during this heist.

Nelson saw a motorcycle patrolman, Hale Keith, through the window. He stood on a cashier's counter and fired his gun, laughing while he shot. Nelson hit the man several times. Luckily Keith survived, but this violent and entirely unprovoked attack was unprecedented for a Dillinger Gang robbery. Other shootings had at least been ostensibly in self-defense, or to serve a purpose. They didn't shoot innocent people. But Nelson just enjoyed chaos.

Taking the $49,500 they scored from the bank, the gang surrounded themselves with hostages and bystanders on the way to their car. The waiting police didn't dare attempt to take out any gang members when they were so close to innocent civilians. The gang made five of their hostages stand on the car's running boards to create a human shield as they drove away.

One Officer managed to shoot the car's radiator before the gang drove out of sight. This slowed the car down a few miles outside of town. Three police cars caught up to them, but retreated in the ensuing hail of gunfire. The gang hijacked another vehicle, drove the hostages ten miles out of town, released them, and escaped.

Despite the chaotic robbery and close call with the police, the Second Dillinger Gang immediately began planning another robbery. On March 13th, 1934, just a week after the Sioux Falls heist, the gang hit First National Bank in Mason City, Iowa. Again, Nelson caused trouble. He, Carroll and

Dillinger were stationed outside the bank, while the other men went in to collect the money.

Nelson was firing wildly in different directions for no obvious reason. He ended up hitting bystander R.L James in the leg. Later, when Hamilton came out of the bank he was enraged seeing another innocent person wounded. Nelson, obviously lying, claimed he thought the man was a police officer.

Though his shots were the most arbitrary and destructive, Nelson was far from the only one to fire a gun that day. An off-duty police officer, James Buchanan, saw what was happening at the bank. He grabbed a sawed-off shotgun and took cover nearby.

He didn't want to fire into the crowd that that gathered to watch the robbery, so he just traded insults with Dillinger, who was guarding the bank door.

Something Buchanan said must have rubbed Dillinger the wrong way. That or he just got bored of the interaction. Dillinger pulled his .38 pistol from his pocket and fired, missing Buchanan. Carroll also fired his weapon at an oncoming car that quickly backed up and fled the scene.

All the gunfire caught the attention of Judge John C. Shipley who was working in his third floor office above the bank. He appeared at the window to see what the commotion was, and Dillinger fired up a volley of shots to warn Shipley to keep out of it. Shipley went to his desk, retrieved his pistol, and shot Dillinger in the shoulder.

After the men left the bank with $52,000, Shipley once again fired at the gang members. This time he managed to hit Hamilton, also in the shoulder. Like the Sioux Falls robbery, the gang managed to get away thanks to a human shield of hostages. Dillinger and Hamilton visited Dr, Nels Mortensen in the middle of the night to have their wounds attended to.

Lincoln Court Shootout

On March 20th 1934, Dillinger moved into the Lincoln Court Apartments in St. Paul, Minnesota, with his girlfriend, Evelyn "Billie" Frechette. The couple used the aliases Mr. and Mrs. Carl T. Hellman.

The Lincoln Court landlady, Daisy Coffey, was immediately suspicious of the couple. They often had parties that would last all night, and were frequently visited by other suspicious individuals. Coffey said she spent much of the Hellmans' stay in apartment 310, which allowed her to look into their apartment, number 303, from across the courtyard.

Eventually Coffey decided to let the Minnesota branch of the Bureau of Investigation know of the odd happenings in apartment 303. Lincoln Court was then put under surveillance by Agent Rufus Coulter, and Agent Rusty Nalls.

On March 31st, 1934 the two agents, along with St. Paul police detective Henry Cummings, continued to surveil the complex, looking for the Hudson sedan Coffey had made note of to the Bureau.

Coulter and Cummings then went up to apartment 303 to talk to the suspicious tenants. Billie Frechette answered the door, cracking it only a few inches. She told the men she wasn't dressed and they would have to wait a few minutes. Nalls, seated in the car downstairs, saw Homer Van Meter pull up and enter the apartment complex.

Coulter went to use a phone and inform the Bureau of their attempt to engage with whoever was in the apartment. He returned to wait for Billie to open the apartment door, when Van Meter suddenly appeared in the hallway. He evaded the officers' questions and tried to calmly walk back down the stairs. Coulter and Cummings were suspicious of the man, and Coulter followed him to the lobby, where Van Meter opened fire on the agent.

Coulter fled outside where Nalls told him to disable Van Meter's car. Coulter shot out the tires of Van Meter's Ford, but Van Meter still managed to get away, either by hopping on a passing truck, or by carjacking a passerby.

Meanwhile, Billie had realized that the men at the door were law enforcement, and told Dillinger they had been found. After hearing Van Meter's shots from the lobby, Dillinger fired through the door of his apartment into the hallway where Cummings still stood. The officer dove for cover and, when Dillinger came out into the hallway to continue to shoot, Cummings shot back.

There was a significant imbalance of firepower between the men. Dillinger had a Thompson submachine gun, capable of firing off bursts of bullets at a time; while Cummings just had his police revolver that only held five rounds. Cummings shot at

Dillinger, hitting him in the calf with one of his few bullets, and managed to flee down the stairs and out of the building.

Dillinger and Frechette exited the building through a back door, and drove off in their Hudson. They went to Eddie Green's safe house where Dr. Clayton May was called to look at Dillinger's wound. Dillinger was moved to the apartment of Augusta Salt, where May worked on patients he could not see out in the open at his office. He stayed there for five days.

On April 2nd, 1934 Eddie Green visited Dillinger at Salt's apartment. Later that day he would be tracked down and shot by the Bureau of Investigation. He would die of his wounds on April 11th, but not before he made several delirious statements to the Bureau of Investigation.

It was clear that the Bureau of Investigation had a far-reaching influence, and was going to be relentless in their pursuit of Dillinger and his gang. John and Billie decided to go back to Mooresville and stay with John Sr. and reconnect with other Dillinger family members.

Early in the morning of April 7th, John and his half-brother Hubert were in a car accident. The Dillingers were returning from Ohio where they were attempting to visit Harry Pierpont's parents. Hubert fell asleep at the wheel, rammed into another car, and ended up 200 feet in the woods. Both Dillingers fled the scene.

In the car, police found some odd items, including some maps, a length of rope, and a bullwhip. Hubert later said his brother was going to use the bullwhip on his former lawyer, Joseph Ryan, who had disappeared with his retainer.

The party needed a new car. Later that day Billie, Hubert, and Hubert's wife bought a new Ford V8. The next day the Dillingers had a family picnic. The Bureau of Investigation surveilled the picnic. Dillinger knew he was being watched. He escaped by hiding on the floor of Billie's new V8, and having her drive him and several family members from the picnic.

On April 9th, Dillinger and Frechette drove to Chicago to meet up with friends of the

Dillinger Gang, hoping they would help the couple find a safe house. Larry Strong promised to help hide the couple. Larry sent them to his tavern to await details. Billie entered first to make sure it was safe for John. It wasn't. Strong had turned against Dillinger, and police officers were inside the tavern waiting for him. They took Billie into custody.

Dillinger was frantic and panicked knowing he couldn't go into the tavern to help Billie as he would either be arrested along with her, or killed on the spot. He immediately hired his lawyer, Louis Piquett, to take on Billie's case, and often met with him to discuss it.

Billie was given a $1,000 fine, and was sentenced to two years in prison for harboring a fugitive. Dillinger paid her fine for her, though Piquett claimed the money came from Billie's sister, as the very fugitive Billie was in trouble for harboring paying the fine she incurred for harboring him would not look good for her.

John desperately wanted to break Billie out of prison, even going as far as casing to the prison to get a feel of the layout, and robbing a police arsenal in Warsaw, Indiana with Van Meter to acquire the firepower necessary to stage a breakout. Billie and Dillinger's other friends managed to convince him he shouldn't attempt a rescue. He would surely be recognized, and probably killed, if he approached the prison, or made any trouble.

Dillinger and his gang, along with the wives and girlfriends of the members decided to go into hiding somewhere nice and remote where they could all unwind and Dillinger could get his mind off Billie's arrest.

Little Bohemia Lodge

On April 20th, 1934, the whole of the Second Dillinger Gang (Dillinger, Van Meter, Nelson, Carroll, Hamilton, their wives and girlfriends, and gang errand runner Pat Reilly) checked into Little Bohemia Lodge in Manitowish Waters, Wisconsin.

The gang was planning on having a quiet weekend of dining and card playing. They were not to get their wish. The lodge owner, Emil Wanatka, felt something was amiss during a game of cards he was playing with Dillinger, Nelson, and Hamilton. When Dillinger won a hand and stood up to collect his winnings, Wanatka noticed the man wore a shoulder holster. Looking around at his other guests, he saw the rest were similarly armed.

While out in town the next day, Wanatka's wife told a friend, Henry Voss, that they believed The Dillinger Gang was staying at their lodge. Voss called the Bureau to inform them of the whereabouts of the gang, and the layout of Little Bohemia.

Melvin Purvis, not wanting to waste any time, or let the gang get away, immediately mobilized a team to fly from Chicago to Wisconsin. The team planned to simply sneak up to the lodge, and take the gang by surprise. There weren't many roads into the lodge, and the building backed out onto a lake, so Purvis assumed there wouldn't be many ways for gang members to escape the raid.

This was the very early days of the Bureau. There were not yet protocols to follow for this type of raid. No roadblocks had been set up, the local authorities were not informed, and the agents were not completely sure of the layout of the lodge, or who exactly was meant to be there.

That night Little Bohemia Lodge was having a dinner special that attracted around 75 people. Some guests were still leaving just as the agents were driving up. A car leaving the lodge approached the agents, who shouted at the driver to stop and identify himself. The men in the car, John Hoffman, Eugene Boisneau and John Morris, didn't hear the command due to the volume of the radio, and their boisterous conversation.

The agents opened fire on the car, killing Boisneau, and wounding Morris and Hoffman. At that moment, Pat Reilly and a gang member girlfriend Pat Cherrington, were returning from an errand Reilly was running for Van Meter. They saw the trouble with the civilian car and made a hasty break for freedom. The agents shot at Reilly and Cherrington, but the two managed to get away.

All the commotion outside alerted the gang members to the presence of authorities. Dillinger, Van Meter, Hamilton, and Carroll all fled on foot through the back of the lodge and into the woods.

Baby Face Nelson, not being one to shy away from a fight, got into a shootout with the agents. He fled into the woods in the opposite direction of the rest of the gang.

Nelson emerged from the woods just a mile away from the lodge. He kidnapped a couple and forced them to drive him away. Shortly after this he ordered them to pull over again, and entered the home of Alvin Koerner, who had already reported the suspicious car idling outside of his house.

Emil Wanatka and his brother-in-law, George LaPorte, were driving to Koerner's house to borrow coats and supplies for the workers of Little Bohemia, who were being forced to stand around outside in the parking lot due to the raid.

Nelson attempted to take more hostages and steal yet another car. He forced Wanatka and Koerner into LaPorte's car and demanded to be driven away. The car stalled, and Wanatka could not get it to start.

As the men tried to get the car to work again, and Nelson became increasingly agitated, a Bureau vehicle drove up. Agents W. Carter Baum and Jay Newman, and local police officer Carl Christensen were in the car. They were responding to Koerner's tip about the suspicious vehicle parked outside his house.

Nelson asked the men to identify themselves. When they told him they were agents he demanded they get out of the car. Newman and Christensen began to get out of the car, and Nelson opened fire on them.

He shot Newman in the forehead, hit Christensen several times, sending him into a ditch, and fatally wounded Baum with three shots to the neck.

Koerner and Wanatka got out of LaPorte's car and ran for cover. Nelson began firing wildly in different directions attempting to shoot his hostages. He then shot Christensen and Newman again. He hopped into the awaiting Bureau vehicle, and pushed Baum's body out onto the ground before driving away.

Purvis was sure Dillinger and his gang was still hiding somewhere in Little Bohemia. As the sun rose, shining light on Wanatka's bullet-ridden lodge, he told Purvis the gang was sure to have all escaped during the night.

Agents took Nelson's wife Helen, as well as Marie Comforti, and Jean Delaney into custody. They were all found guilty of harboring known criminals, but were released on parole.

Dillinger, Van Meter, and Hamilton all rendezvoused after their escape and managed to commandeer a vehicle. Minnesota police received a tip that the gang might be heading in their direction. They were given a license plate number and car model to watch for. The car was spotted at around 10am, April 23rd, 1934 in St. Paul Minnesota.

St. Paul authorities Joe Heinen, Norman Dieters, Larry Dunn, and Fred McArdle followed the vehicle south to St. Paul Park. There the authorities fired warning shots at Dillinger, Van Meter, and Hamilton. Dillinger fired back, and a chase ensued. Fifty shots were fired altogether, including one by McArdle that severely wounded Hamilton.

Famous underworld doctor, Joseph Moran, refused to treat Hamilton, though he did allow him to use the Barker-Karpis safe house to recuperate. Hamilton died of his wounds on April 27th, and was buried in a gravel pit in Oswego, Illinois by Dillinger, Van Meter, and friends.

Public Enemy #1

The raid on Little Bohemia Lodge was catastrophic for the Bureau of Investigation and for Hoover and Purvis personally. With one Bureau agent, and one civilian dead, many others wounded, and no gang members in custody, the whole operation was a huge disaster. Calls went out for Hoover's resignation and Purvis' suspension. Hoover had to up the efforts to find Dillinger and his murderous companions.

The term Public Enemy first appeared in American law enforcement in April 1930, when Chicago Crime Commission chairman Frank J. Loesch attempted to organize the many gangsters who were popping up during Al Capone's reign in Chicago.

He said of the invention of the list, "I had the operating director of the Chicago Crime Commission bring before me a list of the outstanding hoodlums, known murderers, murderers which you and I know but can't prove, and there were about one hundred of them, and out of this list I selected twenty-eight men. I put Al Capone at the head and his brother next, and ran down the twenty-eight, every man being really an outlaw. I called them Public Enemies, and so designated them in my letter, sent to the Chief of Police, the Sheriff [and] every law enforcing officer. The purpose is to keep the publicity light shining on Chicago's most prominent, well known and notorious gangsters to the end that they may be under constant observation by the law enforcing authorities and law-abiding citizens."

It was not meant to be a list of people who were actively wanted by authorities for known crimes, just a list of people who were known criminals, and who should be watched. When J. Edgar Hoover became director of the Bureau of Investigation he appropriated the phrase, and used it to designate the fugitives he most wanted to have in custody, or dead. In 1950, list would become the Ten Most Wanted Fugitives List.

After the disastrous shootout at Little Bohemia, with his career hanging in the balance, Hoover decided to prioritize the Bureau's Public Enemies. The story goes that

Dillinger was given the designation of the Bureau's first Public Enemy Number One on his 31st birthday. "Pretty Boy" Floyd would replace Dillinger after his death, who would then be replaced by Dillinger's crime colleague Baby Face Nelson.

The heat was on like never before. The entire country was looking for Dillinger, Hamilton had just died, and Nelson had yet to return from his escape after Little Bohemia. This left Dillinger, Van Meter, and Carroll to have to scrounge up some money to evade the law by themselves. So they did what they did best.

Van Meter knew of a town in Ohio that was so unlike their usual hits they probably wouldn't even be suspected of the crime.

Fostoria was a railroad town that had as many as 140 trains slowly making their way through the center of town on a daily basis. Meticulous bank robbers like Herman Lamm would never plan a heist in a town that was practically inescapable.

Van Meter, though, had spent summers in the town as a child as was sure he knew the routes around town that would avoid the train tracks. He, Dillinger, and Carroll ditched their previous vehicle; blood-stained from Hamilton's shooting, in Chicago, hoping it would further throw off authorities.

They stole another car and made their way to Fostoria, Ohio. It was one of their most dangerous robberies yet. The men had learned to work in a five or six man team, but now they only had three, they also didn't do a test run, or know the layout of the bank, and the town was covered in train tracks where a train could block their escape route at every turn. But the men needed money and, as Van Meter said, if they pulled it off they probably wouldn't even be suspected.

Carroll was the getaway driver for this robbery, leaving Dillinger and Van Meter to go in alone. They were used to having lookouts at the door, and at least one other man in the building for crowd control. Not having cased the bank beforehand, the men didn't know there were two more exits inside the bank, one going to a jeweler store, and one to a drugstore.

A hostage, Frances Hillyard, managed to use one of the exits to escape the robbery, and she ran to find Frank Culp, the Chief of Police. Culp entered the lobby of the bank, hoping to use the mezzanine to fire down on the robbers. Van Meter noticed his entry, though, and immediately shot Culp in the chest with his machine gun.

Carroll heard shots from down the street where he waited in the getaway car. He got out and began firing wildly in the direction of the bank. Two civilians, Robert Shields, and R.W Powley, are hit by his barrage. Townspeople, who once delighted in watching a bank robbery happen, and thought of the outlaws as heroes, now gathered and shot at the men with their own guns.

Using their favorite escape tactic, Van Meter and Dillinger take two hostages, Bill Daub and Ruth Harris, and force them to accompany them outside, stand on the running boards of the car, and be their human shields until they get safely out of town.

The men made off with just over $17,000. Van Meter ended up being right when he said the authorities probably wouldn't even suspect the Dillinger Gang of the robbery, at least not initially.

Dillinger and Van Meter bought a red Ford truck with some of their heist money. They used it as a mobile safe house. Allegedly they outfitted it with mattresses in the back, and actually lived in it for several weeks, splitting their time between the truck and a dilapidated shack in the woods.

On the night of May 24th, 1934, Dillinger and Van Meter were driving the truck through a back road in East Chicago, Indiana, when a pair of policemen drove up. Van Meter decided there was no escaping the situation, and it was a choice between getting sent to jail, and shooting their way out.

He gunned Officers Martin O'Brien and Lloyd Mulvihill down with his Tommy gun before the men even had a chance to reach for their weapons, or exit the car. Their bodies were found later that day. Police just assumed it was the work of the Dillinger Gang because of the distinctive spray of machine gun bullets. The papers even reported that the man were "Slain in Dillinger Style"

One officer also noted that the dead men worked with Officer O'Malley and would be witnesses at Dillinger's murder trial if he were ever caught. This fact lent more credence to the idea that Dillinger shot the officers in cold blood. Dillinger later expressed remorse about this killing, saying they were just officers doing their jobs and they didn't deserve to die. Though, knowing it was him and Van Meter or the officers, it's unlikely he really regretted their deaths. He most likely saw them as unfortunate but necessary collateral damage.

Plastic Surgery

It was clear that the authorities were closing in on Dillinger. With these latest murders he was officially being blamed for crimes that police weren't even sure he committed. He needed to do something drastic. He asked his lawyers, Louis Piquett and Arthur O'Leary to find him a reliable plastic surgeon to alter his face enough that he would no longer be recognized.

On May 27th Dillinger moved into James Probasco's house. Probasco was a former boxer and member of a diamond heist ring. He was briefly trained as a veterinarian in his youth and now had a makeshift operating room in his home.

Piquett and O'Leary reached out to underworld doctor William Loeser, and his assistant Doctor Harold Cassidy. Both men had been in and out of trouble with the law for various reasons and needed the money they would get from the surgery.

Probasco had set the price of using his operating room and helping the lawyers finds the surgeons at $5,000 (over $90,000 in today's currency). Probasco had promised Loeser $1,700, while Cassidy was to get $1,200.

On May 28th the surgeons came to Probasco's house to begin surgery on Dillinger. John lied about how much he had eaten that day. This lead to the failure of the first attempt at anesthetizing Dillinger. In

Cassidy's second attempt he poured the entire bottle of ether onto the rag. Dillinger lost consciousness, but almost lost his life, too. He stopped breathing and began to turn blue before some primitive CPR tactics were used by Dr. Loeser which brought Dillinger back from the brink of death.

The surgery was brutal. Dillinger kept waking up from the anesthesia and vomiting, both from the ether overdose and the pure shock of being awake during a surgery. Over the course of several hours the doctors removed three moles from Dillinger's face, gave him a rudimentary face-lift, and filled in his famous cleft chin.

The doctors did what they could, but considering they were working in a makeshift operating room, not a hospital, and plastic surgery was actually relatively new at the time, they couldn't work miracles. However, Dillinger was initially pleased enough with the surgery to convince Van Meter to hand over his own $5,000 for the same procedure.

Later, once the swelling went down and he was mostly healed, Dillinger allegedly said, "Hell, I don't look any different than I did!"

The men soon realized they had another problem. Under the guidance of J. Edgar Hoover, America now had a centralized data bank of criminal fingerprints. It was the first era in history where your fingerprints could lead to your capture and arrest. This was bad news for Dillinger and Van Meter. Luckily for them, Dr. Loeser had recently invented a system of fingerprint removal.

He used a combination of nitric and hydrochloric acids in an excruciating procedure for which he charged the men an additional $100 per finger. After Dillinger's death, Loeser was found and made to testify about the work he did on Dillinger and Van Meter.

He described the fingerprint removal saying, "Cassidy and I worked on Dillinger and Van Meter simultaneously on June 3. While the work was being done, Dillinger and Van Meter changed off. The work that could be done while the patient was sitting up, that patient was in the sitting-room. The work that had to be done while the man was lying down, that patient was on the couch in the bedroom. They were changed back and forth according to the work to be done. The hands were sterilized, made aseptic with antiseptics, thoroughly washed with soap and water and used sterile gauze afterwards to keep them clean. Next, cutting instrument, knife was used to expose the lower skin...in other words, take off the epidermis and expose the derma, then alternately the acid and the alkaloid was applied as was necessary to produce the desired results."

Dillinger's autopsy showed that the procedure didn't completely work, and his fingerprints, while not completely intact, were still partially visible.

The Last Days of the Dillinger Gang

A few days after Dillinger and Van Meter's fingerprint surgeries, Tommy Carroll went to Waterloo, Iowa with his girlfriend, Jean Delaney. On June 7th, the couple stopped to gas up their car, then went to lunch. The gas station attendant had noticed several out-of-state license plates in the back seat, and reported the suspicious fact to the local police, along with the make and model of the car, and its current license number.

Detectives Emil Steffen and P.E. Walker drove around looking for the vehicle but had no luck until they returned to the station. Carroll had mistakenly parked across the street from the local police station. Carroll put up a fight when the detectives tried to arrest him and ended up getting shot four times. He later died of his wounds in St. Francis Hospital. Delaney, having been one of the women taken into custody after the Little Bohemia shootout, was arrested for violating her parole and given a year in jail.

All but three members of the Second Dillinger Gang were now dead and Dillinger feared the rest of them would be following closely behind their colleagues. With their funds depleted by the surgeries, and their eyes on a comfortable retirement in a tropical location, the gang planned one more big robbery.

Van Meter chose the Merchants National Bank in South Bend, Indiana. Done at the right time he figured the men could make off with $100,000. As many as three other men were brought on for the heist. Their identities have never been conclusively proven, though some speculate one could have been "Pretty Boy" Floyd, the man who took Dillinger's place as Public Enemy Number One after his death.

On June 30th, 1934 the men descended on South Bend. Van Meter was on lookout that day, while the others made their way into the bank. One of the unidentified men immediately began shooting up at the ceiling. The noise from the bank prompted Officer Howard Wagner to investigate. Van Meter saw him coming and shot him before he had the chance to get to the bank. He died on the scene.

The shooting set off a panic in the street. It was chaos as people ran for safety. Van Meter could hear sirens in the distance. Harry Berg, a local shop owner, grabbed his pistol from his shop and shot at one of the robbers.

Berg managed to hit Nelson who was not wounded due to his bulletproof vest, but was characteristically impulsive. He swung around and began firing wildly in the direction of the shooter. Many bullets shattered shop windows and car windshields. Bystanders were grazed with bullets and showered in shards of glass.

Joseph Pawlowski, a teenager who was passing by the scene, jumped on Nelson's back to try and stop him from shooting.

Nelson struggled free, slamming Pawlowski into a glass window. The boy was shot in the hand by a stray bullet and passed out.

Police arrived on the scene and bullets continued to fly from both sides. The shootout racked up thousands of dollars in property damage, and wounded six civilians. Van Meter was grazed in the head by a police bullet. Dillinger and the gang got away as they usually did, by taking hostages from the bank. Among the hostages this time was the bank president.

The heist was not as fruitful as Van Meter had hoped. Not only did he get shot in the head, and murder a man, the gang only managed to steal $29,890, over $70,000 less than he was expecting.

The South Bend robbery ended up being the last recorded robbery for everyone known to have been, and suspected to have been involved. Less than a month later, Dillinger would be dead.

Betrayal and Death

After Billie's incarceration, John started dating 26-year-old Polly Hamilton, a waitress, and former prostitute at the brothel of Anna Sage. Hamilton and Sage stayed close, and were even living together at the time, along with Sage's son.

Anna Sage was actually Ana Cumpănaş, a Romanian madam, who ran a brothel in Gary, Indiana. She was being threatened with deportation for "low moral character". Desperate to find a way to stay in the country, Sage decided she would give the authorities what information she had on Dillinger.

Whether Sage knew her information would lead to Dillinger's death is unclear. It is certain, though, that she is the one who gave up Dillinger's location to authorities on the night he was killed.

She told Bureau agents that she, Polly, and Dillinger would be going to see a film on July 22nd, 1934. She was unsure whether the trio would go to the Biograph or Marbro theatre, but promised to get the information to the agents before the film. She also told them she would be wearing an orange dress, so they could more easily identify her, and thus, Dillinger.

When the day came, Sage, Hamilton, and Dillinger were spending time at Sage's house. She asked Dillinger where he wanted to go to the movie later, and he told her he wanted to go to the theater around the corner, meaning the Biograph.

Sage didn't have a phone, and wouldn't be able to make such a delicate phone call within earshot of Dillinger anyway. She told the couple she needed to quickly run to the store to get some butter for the fried chicken she was making for dinner. At the store, she called Melvin Purvis to inform him of the evening's plan.

Purvis and Hoover began mobilizing their men. Even with the tip from Sage they still thought it best to send agents to both theaters. They couldn't be totally sure that Sage was telling the truth, or that Dillinger wouldn't change his mind about what theater he wanted to go to. They wanted to leave no room for mistakes. Purvis and Hoover were fully determined to not let Dillinger slip through their fingers again.

At 8:30pm Dillinger, Hamilton, and Sage entered the Biograph Theater to see Clark Gable in the crime film Manhattan Melodrama. The studio later used the fact that Dillinger was taken out after he saw their film in order to promote it; a real-life crime drama coming to an end just steps away from their fictitious one.

Once they were sure Dillinger was in the Biograph, Purvis pulled the team from the Marbro Theater for extra manpower at the Biograph. Nobody wanted to risk letting Dillinger escape.

The Chicago police were not informed of the Bureau's plan to take down Dillinger. Purvis and Hoover not only wanted the glory for themselves, they also considered the Chicago PD to be inept, or possibly under Dillinger's thumb.

Some Chicago officers still showed up to the scene, though. They were called by a theater employee who, seeing so many men surrounding the theater, thought they were planning a robbery. Bureau agents had to quickly explain they were waiting on an important target, and that an obvious police presence might compromise the whole operation.

After the film Purvis waited in the doorway of the theater. Seeing Sage's orange dress as she, Polly, and Dillinger walked by, Purvis signaled the other agents by lighting a cigar. Many accounts say Dillinger looked Purvis right in the eye as he passed. He must have recognized the man who had been hunting him down for months because he then began to break away from Sage and Hamilton, and reach into his pocket for his pistol.

Dillinger made a break away from his dates and into a nearby alleyway. The Bureau had already blocked off this means of escape, but Dillinger was not about to just surrender to the authorities. Acting on orders to open fire on their target if he resisted arrest, three agents began shooting at Dillinger.

Herman Hollis, Clarence Hurt, and Charles Winstead all fired shots at Dillinger. In all the three men fired six bullets; Dillinger was shot four times and grazed twice. The bullet that killed him entered through the base of his neck, went through his spinal cord and brain, and exited just below his right eye. Dillinger fell on face first onto the ground.

An ambulance arrived shortly after the shooting, although it was clear Dillinger was already dead. He was officially pronounced dead at Alexian Brothers Hospital at 10:40pm, on July 22nd, 1934.

As a testament to his popularity, civilians on the scene supposedly dipped their handkerchiefs and skirt hems into Dillinger's blood as a souvenir. An estimated 15,000 people went to the Cook County morgue to visit his body, which was on display there for only a day and a half.

Rumors started to swirl that the man killed that night was not, in fact, John Dillinger. How could America's most notorious outlaw, a man who had escaped from jail twice, and evaded federal agents countless times, be brought down in such simple circumstances? People pointed to the difference in various facial features between pictures of Dillinger when he was alive, and what he looked like in death.

Of course, at the time, people may not have known that John underwent a crude plastic surgery in the hopes that he might be misidentified.

Only July 24th, Dillinger's body was sent back to his family in Indiana. Allegedly the hearse occasionally stopped along the way to display Dillinger's body to curious crowds. On July 25th, Dillinger's sister, Audrey, officially identified the body. John was given a funeral service, and was then buried in the family plot in Crown Hill Cemetery in Indianapolis, Indiana. There are still those who believe John Dillinger was not killed that night.

Dillinger's grave marker has had to be replaced three times since he was laid to rest, due to outlaw fans chipping pieces off of it to keep as a reminder of the legend buried beneath.

Conclusion

With Dillinger dead, the Outlaw Era was quickly coming to an end. Famous bank robbing duo Bonnie and Clyde were shot to death just two months before Dillinger.

Neither Baby Face Nelson, nor Homer Van Meter would survive until the end of the year, either. Van Meter was cornered by St. Paul authorities Chief Frank Cullen, Detective Tom Brown, and two other officers on August 23rd, 1934. He ran into an alleyway and fired two shots at the approaching men with his .45 caliber pistol. He was then riddled with bullets from police rifles and even submachine guns, prompting Van Meter's family to claim he was used as "target practice". He was buried in Fort

Wayne, Indiana, though the family did not give him a space in their family plot because of the shame he had brought to the Van Meter name.

Baby Face Nelson died the way he lived, in a violent and bloody gun battle. On November 27th, 1934, Nelson, his wife Helen, and an accomplice, John Paul Chase were driving on a highway near Chicago, when a Bureau vehicle housing agents Thomas McDade and William Ryan passed by, travelling in the opposite direction. Nelson and the agents recognized each other and began a bizarre pursuit that ended in Nelson tailing the agents instead of attempting to get away.

Another Bureau vehicle spotted Nelson and began pursuing him. In this vehicle was

Agent Samuel P. Cowley, and Agent Herman Hollis, one of the three men who fired at Dillinger on the day he died. Nelson had Helen drive to Barrington Park. The Bureau vehicle followed, and The Battle of Barrington began. By the end of the ensuing gun battle, Nelson and Hollis would be dead. Cowley died a few hours later from his wounds.

Like Tommy Carroll's girlfriend Jean Delaney, Helen Gillis had been arrested and released on parole after the Little Bohemia shootout. She was given a year in prison for harboring her husband.

From then on there was a shift in the minds of the American people. With most of the once-revered outlaws dead or in jail, and the threat of fascism looming over the world, people began to look at good and evil differently. Where they once saw outlaws as heroes who were standing up to the rich institutions that were stealing money from poor citizens, Americans now looked on outlaws as murderous criminals; relics of a bygone era.

The Federal Bureau of Investigation as we know it today was officially created out of the Bureau of Investigation and the Division of Investigation in 1935, partly due to the agents' stellar work catching and killing their Public Enemies.

The legend of John Dillinger has lived on in media portrayals since almost immediately following his death. The 1935 MGM film

Public Hero No. 1 included many details from Dillinger's life, including the shootout at Little Bohemia, a crude plastic surgery, and a shooting death in an alleyway outside a theater.

Many other films have been made about Dillinger's life since, including the most recent Public Enemies from 2009, starring Johnny Depp as John Dillinger.

The stories of these men and their other outlaw counterparts continue to fascinate people to this day. Perhaps people still see them as Robin Hood-type anti-heroes undermining the corrupt establishment. Maybe people long for a time when crime was almost elegant; committed by men and women with professionalism and style.

Regardless, the legendary John Dillinger will not soon be forgotten.

Al Capone

American Gangster Stories

Roger Harrington

Humble Beginnings

Although he ultimately became notorious as a crime boss engaged in bootlegging, gambling and various other illegal activities and was named by the Chicago Crime Commission as 'Public Enemy Number 1', Al Capone's beginnings were decidedly humble.

Alphonse Gabriel Capone was born on 17th January 1899 in Brooklyn, New York City. Although many people turn to crime to escape their poor background, this wasn't really the case with Al Capone. His parents were respectable people who emigrated from Italy to Austria-Hungary (now Croatia) in 1893 and then by ship to the U.S.

Father Gabriele was employed as a barber while mother Teresa worked for some time as a seamstress. When they arrived in America, they already had two sons and Teresa was pregnant with a third child. They lived initially in a squalid tenement building near the Navy Yard, a generally rough and noisy area although the family managed to remain normal and law-abiding.

Al Capone was born the fourth of nine children, one of whom died at the age of one. Two brothers, Rafaela James (known as 'Ralph') and Salvatore (or 'Frank'), eventually joined Al in his criminal activities. Ironically, given Capone's later career, one brother — Vincenzo, who changed his name to Richard Hart — became a prohibition agent.

Unhappy Schooldays

Capone attended a strict Catholic school where he struggled with the rules and the brutality he faced there. Despite this, he was a promising pupil at least at first. This all changed, however, when he was expelled at the age of fourteen for hitting a female teacher in the face.

The boy's formal education ended at this point and his descent into a criminal career had begun. The transition was no doubt also helped by the family's move, when he was aged eleven, to Park Slope in Brooklyn. This was a much more ethnically mixed area of New York and it resulted in Capone being affected by wider cultural influences.

Included among those influences was Capone's membership of several local gangs. He initially joined the Junior Forty Thieves and then moved on to the Bowery Boys, the Brooklyn Rippers, James Street Boys Gang and eventually the powerful Five Points Gang in Lower Manhattan. The latter was run by gangster Johnny Torrio, who was to have a huge influence on Capone's life.

Early Career

After being expelled from school, Capone took on various odd jobs in the Brooklyn area, including working in a bowling alley and a candy store. Full-time work followed, primarily at the Harvard Inn on Coney Island, owned by mobster Frankie Yale, where Capone worked as a bartender and bouncer.

Whilst working there, Capone inadvertently insulted a woman patron, resulting in her brother, Frank Gallucio, slashing him across the face with a knife in retribution. This caused three prominent scars on the left side of his face that resulted in the press nicknaming him 'Scarface'. After that, Capone always tried to present the other side of his face to cameras and described his scars as 'war wounds', despite never serving in the military.

On Frankie Yale's insistence, Capone apologised to Gallucio for insulting his sister. Nevertheless, he appeared not to bear a grudge since he later hired Gallucio as his bodyguard.

Becoming a Married Man

On 30th December 1918, aged only nineteen, Capone married Irish Catholic Mae Josephine Coughlin. Since he was under 21 at the time, he required the written permission of his parents before the wedding could go ahead. The couple remained married until his death and had one child,

Albert Francis 'Sonny' Capone, who was born just prior to their marriage.

The marriage appeared to change Capone, if only temporarily, and he reportedly worked for a period as a bookkeeper. Within little more than a year, however, he was off to Chicago to work for old associate Johnny Torrio and his career as a criminal really took off.

Moving On

The reasons for Capone's move to Chicago from New York in 1920 are somewhat unclear. There is a belief that the unexpected death of his father prompted a change while there were stories that there was a need to get out after severely injuring a rival gang member. More likely is that he went at the request of Johnny Torrio, for whom he'd worked when aged only fifteen, since he immediately became employed by him on arriving there.

At the time, Torrio operated as an enforcer for crime boss James 'Big Jim' Colosimo. When Colosimo was murdered on 11th May 1920, with the culprits rumored to be either

Capone or Frankie Yale, Torrio took over the business.

Capone initially worked as a bouncer in a brothel. Here he contracted syphilis, which went untreated because the symptoms subsided and he wrongly assumed the disease had somehow been cured. It returned with a vengeance later and was to eventually lead to the deterioration in his physical and mental health that ultimately contributed to his early death.

Opportunities Abound

The start of the Prohibition era in 1920 offered great opportunities to make immense amounts of money from illegal bootlegging operations. And Chicago was ideally located to capitalize on these opportunities, being well served by railroads and with easy access to huge areas of the USA and Canada.

Added to that, Chicago was a city that had grown from a mere 30,000 people in 1850 to around three million when Capone arrived. The influx of all types and nationalities provided a ready market for what he was supplying.

Although Colosimo had been active in operating many brothels and gambling dens in the city, he had supposedly wanted nothing to do with bootlegging. Torrio, however, had no such qualms and, on taking over, went into bootlegging in a big way.

Capone's business sense led to him taking over the running of the Four Deuces, a whorehouse, speakeasy and gambling joint that was also Torrio's headquarters. The basement area was reputedly used to torture opponents and those with useful information. Capone soon became Torrio's right-hand man, helping to run the biggest organised crime group in Chicago.

Torrio had a reputation as a 'gentleman gangster' and his style was to avoid conflict with rival gangs, instead preferring to negotiate with them over territory agreements. These attempts failed in the case of Dean O'Banion, the leader of the smaller North Side Gang, whose territory was increasingly threatened by the Genna brothers and apparently with Torrio's blessing.

On Torrio's orders or agreement, O'Banion was murdered on 24th October 1924. O'Banion's close friend Hymie Weiss took over the North Side Gang and made revenge over the killing a priority. That resulted in an unsuccessful attempt on Capone's life in January 1925 and Torrio being shot multiple times twelve days later.

Capone's Ascension to Gang Boss

Although Torrio recovered from his injuries, he retired and handed over full control to Capone. He returned to his native Italy for a period of three years before eventually coming back to the US.

At the age of 26, Al Capone was in charge of an organization, which he referred to as the 'Outfit' that included gambling, prostitution and illegal breweries backed up by a transport network that spread across America and into Canada.

All of that came with protection from law enforcement agencies and politicians, together with a degree of ignorance — some newspapers describing him as a 'boxing promoter' due to him having promoted local fights in order to raise extra money. Capone marked his elevation by increasing the organization's revenue through the use of uncompromising tactics.

Any businesses that refused to deal with him were treated harshly. That generally meant their property being blown up, around one hundred people losing their lives during the 1920s to these bombings.

Capone's hardline approach meant that the power vacuum usually associated with a gang boss's demise never happened. He quickly smashed all the opposition that would otherwise have been fighting for control and established a supremacy that few dared threaten.

In the event, the outcome was a significant increase in brothels and a business that generated revenue of as much as $100 million annually, equivalent to around $1.2 billion today. Capone had in place a network of brothels and speakeasies throughout the city and controlled the sale of alcohol to more than 10,000 speakeasies. By 1929, his personal net worth had risen to over $40 million — a figure that equates to about $550 million at today's values.

Gaining Influence

In order to gain the protection of Chicago city hall for his bootlegging operations, Capone is widely believed to have helped Republican William Hale Thompson gain election as mayor. By 1923, having put up with the corruption of Thompson as well as his alliance with Torrio for eight years, Chicago elected reformer William Dever as his successor. Fearing a crackdown on his operations, Torrio decided a second base was needed and sent Capone to nearby Cicero to establish a presence there.

Building a Political Base

The potential crackdown on racketeering in Chicago brought into focus the importance of increasing protection against the law enforcement agencies. That objective was largely achieved by a combination of bribery and strong-arm tactics.

To protect their gambling dens, brothels and other illegal activities, Capone and Brothers Frank and Ralph attained leading positions in the Cicero city government. This was partly achieved by threatening voters and kidnapping the election workers of their opponents, although Frank was killed in a Chicago police shoot out during this period.

Capone used threats, bribery and violence to move existing gangster gangs aside. This caused a change in political opinion and existing mayor Joseph Klenha, who was up for re-election in April 1924, asked Capone for help. He responded by turning gang members loose on the election.

Klenha's opponent was forced out of his headquarters by gunmen, the challenger for the city clerk's office was pistol whipped and helpers and campaigners were beaten up. Election workers were kidnapped, policemen attacked and voters who were planning to support the opposition were prevented from voting.

The whole election fell into chaos and officials asked for help. As a result, seventy Chicago police officers were deputised and five squads of detectives were sent to Cicero to restore order.

One squad came across three gunmen who included Al and Frank Capone. In the shoot-out that followed, Frank was killed and Al managed to escape unharmed. In common with many such episodes over several years, he was not arrested.

The campaign of violence was effective, however, since Klenha was comfortably re-elected. With Klenha in his pocket, Capone established his headquarters in the Hawthorne Inn and took over the town.

Klenha was again elected in 1928, although this time there was no repeat of the violence due to a large Chicago police presence. By 1932, the electorate had had enough and Klenha was voted out. Capone, however, wasn't overly concerned since by this time he was already serving time for tax evasion.

Back in Chicago, in the 1927 election, Thompson won the backing of Capone, allegedly to the extent of a $250,000 contribution, by campaigning for a wide open city that might even include the re-opening of illegal saloons.

Thompson won by a narrow margin in 1927, helped by a bombing campaign on the 10th April polling day that targeted booths in areas that were thought to support Thompson's rival William Emmett Dever. Also a victim was lawyer Octavius Granadary, who challenged Thompson's candidature for the African-American vote and was shot and killed after being chased through the streets by cars containing armed men.

Capone's bomber, James Belcastro, was charged along with four police officers but all charges were subsequently dropped when witnesses retracted their statements.

Maintaining Authority and Security

For a period, Capone moved his Chicago headquarters to fifty rooms within the luxurious Metropole Hotel. This was a statement of his authority in the knowledge that Mayor Thompson would comply with his wishes. That authority extended to his mobsters carrying official police department issue cards stating that the bearer should be treated with the same courtesy as police officers.

Whilst the actions in connection with the elections served to safeguard Capone's operations, his life was still in danger. Despite this, he was generally unarmed but was always accompanied by a minimum of two bodyguards and even acquired an armor plated car for his protection. He rarely risked travelling during the day, preferring night-time travel as a safer option.

There was also a tendency to get away from Chicago at every opportunity. This often included taking a night train to various cities, booking at the last minute an entire carriage for Capone and his entourage. On arrival at their destination, they'd book into a luxury hotel under assumed names, occupying suites for up to a week.

Creating his Miami Beach Base

In 1928, Capone bought a 14-room house on Palm Island, Florida. It was purchased from beer magnate Clarence Busch for $40,000 and had ten-foot walls behind which Capone could get away from public attention.

It was a place where he could escape Chicago's harsh winters while still being able to direct operations from there, sometimes on the 32-foot cabin cruiser he had acquired. Palm Island was also the place where Capone eventually spent his final days on release from prison.

The purchase of the Florida mansion was partly prompted by a need to break free from the pressures and persecutions of Chicago. It also resulted from a journey between various cities where Capone was greeted at each one by a large police presence and it was made clear he was not welcome there.

Capone liked Florida in general and Miami in particular. This was due to the benign year round weather and the indulgent lifestyle where gambling was everywhere and prohibition was largely ignored.

Planning to establish a base there, he booked into the penthouse suite of the Ponce de Leon Hotel under the name of 'A Costa'. He also rented a house on Miami Beach for his wife and son at a cost of $2,500 per month.

The property was leased under the name of 'Al Brown' as a precaution. Nevertheless, the owners soon found out who the real occupant was and worried about the safety of the building and its contents. Their fears were misplaced because Capone actually upgraded some of the contents to meet his lifestyle needs and ensured all bills related to the property were settled in full.

How the Palm Island Property was Acquired

The Ponce de Leon Hotel was operated by Parker Henderson Junior, who was eager to please and provided favors for Capone, including purchasing a number of guns for him. He also acted as a real estate representative for Capone and helped locate and acquire the Palm Island mansion where he spent his final days.

The mansion was bought on 27th March 1928 but, knowing Capone wouldn't be welcome as a resident, Henderson signed all the papers as though he was the purchaser and owner of the property.

Capone spent $100,000 improving the estate, adding what was at the time the largest privately-owned swimming pool with a filtration system that could handle sea or fresh water. Also added were new garages, a boathouse, decking and gardens. Capone supervised all the work and insisted on the best of everything but, like the house, it was all done in Henderson's name.

To ensure the highest standards of work, Capone treated all his workers well. That included providing them with sumptuous lunches and the result was a renovation project of which he was proud.

It took some time before it was realized who the real owner of the property was. This was despite Henderson transferring the mansion into the name of Mae Capone, Al's wife.

Attempts to Move Capone Out of Florida

Economic events had slowed the property market and a hurricane in 1926 had not helped matters. So it was feared Capone's arrival would make matters worse and turn Miami Beach into a place where people didn't want to come.

Several local groups protested at Capone's presence in Miami, prompting a meeting with the mayor and the Miami Beach city mayor. They appeared satisfied with his explanation that he was there for relaxation and would not cause any trouble.

Although the area was alive with illegal gambling, prostitution and other corrupt activities, to which local officials had turned a blind eye; Capone was accused of bringing in gambling. There was a newspaper-led campaign to get him out and a move by the American League to strip him of his constitutional rights.

The Miami Beach city council tried to sue him while the governor of Florida attempted to have him arrested. This occurred on a few occasions but only resulted in him being jailed once. Constant surveillance failed to curb his activities and endless harassment did not succeed in driving him out. Capone did attempt to improve relationships by hosting a series of goodwill dinners but opinions were too firmly entrenched to change matters much.

Residents campaigned for his removal and various authorities combined with business leaders to support this action. Many of the latter, however, saw Capone's presence as a business opportunity and efforts to move him out failed.

Those attempts included arresting Capone on vagrancy charges in April 1930, a ploy that a Chicago judge repeated in September of the same year. Neither charge succeeded in achieving the desired intent.

Centre of Attention

Although he was undoubtedly a gangster who inflicted pain, suffering and death on many people, Capone didn't really see himself in the same light. He liked to portray himself as a pillar of the community and a benevolent character that helped others, opening soup kitchens during the Depression and making significant donations to numerous charities. That image was, however, the complete opposite of the view of many — particularly the law enforcement agencies.

Well-known for his brutality, Capone was described by the New Yorker in 1928 as 'the greatest gang leader in history'. Against that, he considered himself a gentleman and believed the jobs he provided, criminal though they may be, created an income for people who would otherwise be poor. He liked to be described as some sort of Robin Hood, who gave to the poor at the expense of the rich.

Many people, particularly Italian immigrants, viewed him as a community leader who helped the poor. One of his projects was to provide daily milk to poor Chicago schoolchildren to help prevent rickets. He would send flowers to the funerals of rival gang members and had a reputation for helping people who were in need.

A Sharp Dresser

Capone was a flamboyant character who wore sharp, pin stripe or chalk suits and fedora hats in lighter, contrasting colors, often with a cigar in his mouth, an image on which numerous fictitious gangster characters are based. The suits were in a variety of colors ranging from charcoal through to lighter summer colors, especially when in Florida. The suit lengths were often imported from Italy at a price that was the equivalent of $6,500 each today.

He was generally adorned with gaudy jeweler, which he dispensed with at his trial for tax evasion in order to display a more conservative image. His more human side also extended to a love of fishing, singing and writing music.

Despite his Italian roots and his membership of what was in essence a crime group with a very Italian background, Capone was fiercely American. If at any time he was described as Italian, he would proudly insist that he was born in Brooklyn.

Maintaining a High Profile

He loved his celebrity status and nourished it by always being available to talk to the press. When questioned about his activities, he portrayed himself as a respectable businessman who aimed to satisfy demand and was providing a public service by doing so.

Capone's courting of the press and his quest for publicity were things that later came back to haunt him. In interviews while in prison, he voiced regrets at having spoken so extensively to the press because the high profile that resulted had made him a target and had at the very least accelerated his eventual demise.

As well as associating with the press, Capone attended the opera, ball games and other public events where he generally was greeted with standing ovations and people wishing to shake him by the hand. Numerous attempts to increase his profile included moving the headquarters to the luxurious Metropole Hotel for a time.

For a period of four years, from 1925 to 1929, Capone was the most high profile gangster in the country. He worked hard to cultivate his image as a respectable businessman who cared for the people of Chicago. Throughout that period, however, conflicts between the rival gangs were increasing and the violence was growing, which was at variance with the image Capone strove to promote.

He hated the nickname of 'Scarface' that was given to him by the press, since it didn't fit with the image he wanted to put out. Instead, he preferred close friends' reference to him as 'Snorky', a slang term to describe a sharp dresser, or other criminal associates calling him the 'Big Fellow' or 'Big Al'.

Neither of the latter names referred to his height because, at five foot ten inches, he was little over average height although he was at the very least somewhat corpulent. The reference was more likely to his status as undisputed head of criminal activities in Chicago.

At the height of his fame, around 1927, his notoriety had spread throughout the country and even abroad. Tour buses drove past his headquarters, visitors expected to see him and the police even recruited him to greet a group of Italian aviators on a world tour.

Capone reputedly had a long-held belief that he would have been better selling milk than alcohol since there was a lot less hassle and an enduring demand. He did, in fact, own a dairy farm and sold milk in bottles that were labelled with expiry dates, which is something we accept as a regular occurrence today. Back then, it tied in with his stated wish for all milk sold in Chicago to have expiry dates, resulting from a relative apparently having become ill after drinking old milk and, possibly, simply being part of his wish to be seen as a respectable businessman.

Relationships with his Family

Capone was a devoted family man and tried to keep his home life entirely separate from his criminal activities, an approach advocated by his mentor Johnny Torrio. One theory is that he started or at least escalated his life of crime to provide for his family after his father died when he was only 21. He was devoted to his mother and was in daily contact with her whenever possible.

Although Capone's marriage to Mae endured right through to his death, that doesn't mean he remained faithful to her. His sexual deeds led to his contracting syphilis and he then infected his wife with the disease, never admitting he had contracted it since that would have been an admission of adultery. For the same reason, he never undertook treatment despite suffering flu-like symptoms, rashes and sores as a result of it.

The conflicting views of Al Capone once led to someone describing him as the kind of person who would kiss babies during the day and kill their parents at night while they slept. That probably just about sums up his personality and was reflected in the way he did business, negotiating with a smile on his face but destroying and killing those who refused to do business with him on his terms.

Victims and Events

Throughout Capone's career, a whole string of killings and other unsavory events were linked to his name. He was prone to mood swings and frequent violent outbursts, which with hindsight may have been brought on by the gradually worsening dementia that resulted from his syphilis infection.

According to the Chicago Daily Tribune, 33 people were killed, directly or indirectly, by Capone, while others put the figure as high as 700. The earliest of these killings, on 7th May 1923, was Joe Howard, who attempted to hijack a beer consignment belonging to Johnny Torrio and had attacked Jake 'Greasy Thumb' Guzik, the trusted treasurer and financial expert of the Outfit. There was also suspicion that Capone had been involved in the death of 'Big Jim' Colosimo three years previously.

Removing Rival Gang Leaders

At Torrio's request, Capone was believed to have participated in the killing of North Side Gang leader Dean O'Banion in November 1924. That incident resulted in Torrio being shot in a revenge attack, forcing his retirement and causing Capone's accession to the top job. It also, in October 1926, led to the murder of Earl 'Hymie' Weiss, who succeeded O'Banion as North Street Gang leader and vowed to get Capone.

Weiss was the son of Polish immigrants and had formed the North Side Gang along with

Dean O'Banion and George 'Bugs' Moran. He took over after O'Banion's death and made several attempts on Capone's life in a bid to gain revenge.

There had been a previous attempt on Weiss's life after Capone's driver was tortured and killed. Following that, on 20th September 1926, the North Side Gang made a concerted attempt to murder Capone.

After staging a ploy to draw him to the windows of his Hawthorne Inn headquarters, they then opened fire with machine guns and shotguns. Capone escaped unhurt and, after attempts to call a truce failed, Weiss and a companion were killed and three others injured three weeks later outside the North Side headquarters.

The response was to kidnap and kill the owner of the Hawthorne Inn's restaurant, who was a friend of Capone.

Although no-one was ever charged with Weiss's murder, it was widely thought that Capone's top gunman, Jack McGurn, armed with a machine gun, had been one of the two assailants. Trusted associate Frank Nitti was suspected of being responsible for the planning of the hit.

The Killing of Billy McSwiggin

On 27th April 1926, in an event that became known as the Adonis Club Massacre, Thomas Duffy and James Doherty were killed due to their threats against an attempt by Capone and Frankie Yale to bring large quantities of bootleg whiskey into Chicago.

The killings were undertaken by gunmen armed with machine guns. They drove past in five cars and opened fire as members of a rival gang left the Adonis Club bar.

Caught up in the shooting and also killed was assistant state prosecutor Billy McSwiggin, known as the 'hanging prosecutor'. McSwiggin was well-known for going after bootleggers. He had previously attempted to prosecute Capone for the murder of a rival but without success.

Although Capone was suspected but not arrested due to a lack of evidence, there was a big public outcry. That helped to turn public opinion against him and possibly, to some degree, set in motion events that would eventually lead to his downfall.

After McSwiggin's murder, Capone lay low for almost three months. Eventually, he came out of hiding and presented himself to the police. With insufficient evidence to have any hope of gaining a conviction, they had no option but to let him go, thereby increasing even further his aura of invincibility.

Killing for a Purpose

Capone viewed killing rival gang members as an act of self-defense since he was only doing it to protect his business. Although he rarely took part in the killings himself, there were incidences where he was known or suspected of having taken personal responsibility. One of these occurred on 7th May 1928, when he eliminated three men who had been part of a plot to assassinate him.

Former associates, they were invited to a banquet and plied with food and drink. Lulled into a false sense of security, they were tied to their chairs and then Capone systematically beat them to death with a baseball bat in a scene later replicated in 'The Untouchables' film.

Another dozen killings followed over the next eighteen months. Some of these were to get rid of rivals who were threatening the operation. Others were people who had been brought in to kill Capone, who had a $50,000 bounty put on his head by rival mobsters, while some planned to testify against him or did not support him as required.

Capone was rarely personally involved in the killings but ordered others to carry them out on his behalf. An exception came after an assault on friend and accomplice Jack Guzik, Capone shooting the culprit dead in a bar. An absence of witnesses meant he was never charged with the murder but his reputation grew as a result.

As Chicago became more violent, with drive-by killings increasingly frequent and innocent people caught in the cross-fire, Capone somewhat surprisingly acted as a peacemaker. He succeeded in stopping the killings and violence for around two months by arranging an amnesty between the various gangs. However, this was never likely to last long and normal activities soon resumed with street violence and fighting between the gangs.

The Treachery of Frankie Yale

A big problem was the regular hijacking of Capone's whiskey transports. This was largely blamed on Frankie Yale, Capone's long-time associate who was now seen as a rival having turned against him. This was reportedly after the appointment of Tony Lombardo as president of Unione Sicilana, an organisation that supposedly controlled much of the Italian-American vote and from which Capone's outfit received some of its political protection.

Capone had supported Lombardo's candidacy while Yale had backed Joe Aiello. Once Lombardo took over, Yale disapproved of his actions and received reduced income from the Unione. He decided to recover the shortfall from Capone and, being responsible for the safe passage of Capone's whiskey shipments through New York, he instead began to hijack some of them.

Yale was killed by machine gun fire on 1st July 1928 but not before he had ordered Capone's informant against him to be murdered. A gun used in that murder was subsequently found to be one of those acquired by Parker Henderson Junior for Capone and led to Henderson eventually testifying against Capone at his tax evasion trial

The St. Valentine's Day Massacre

The next and most notorious event of all, the St. Valentine's Day Massacre, occurred on 14th February 1929. The North Side Gang, which was now led by George Clarence 'Bugs' Moran in succession to Vincent Drucci, who had taken over on Hymie Weiss's death and then himself been killed, had long been a problem for Capone.

The violence between the North Side Gang and Torrio's South Side Gang (later to become the Chicago Outfit) really grew when the latter started selling alcohol on the North Side's territory. That ultimately led to the murder of O'Banion outside a flower shop that he owned.

The relationship between Capone and Moran gradually deteriorated, with Moran attacking Capone's premises, hijacking his liquor shipments and killing those associated with him. There were numerous attacks and retaliations, including two attempts on Capone's life by drive-by shootings, a form of attack that Moran made popular.

An attempt on the life of Capone's friend and associate, Jack McGurn, at last prompted some action. The plan was to ambush Bugs Moran at a warehouse and garage that served as the North Side Gang's headquarters. Capone's men kept watch from an apartment across the street and, on the morning of 14th February, signalled that they had seen Moran enter the premises.

Some of Capone's men, in police uniforms and a stolen police car staged a raid on the premises and lined seven men up against a wall without a struggle. They were disarmed and then shot in cold blood with machineguns and shotguns.

Six of the men were killed instantly but one, Frank Gusenberg, was still alive despite having taken fourteen bullets. He made it to the hospital but died shortly afterwards.

The main problem for Capone was that Moran, despite the information given to him, was not among the victims. Having seen the police car pull up outside the warehouse, he had made his getaway before the attack took place. All Capone's further attempts to get Moran failed, the gangster eventually dying of lung cancer while serving the second of two ten-year jail sentences for bank robbery.

Aftermath of the St. Valentine's Day Massacre

The atrocity caused public outrage and prompted intense police activity. Up to that point, people had tolerated Prohibition and the lawlessness that came with it. Most of the associated violence revolved around gangsters shooting other gangsters, with usually no direct effect on the general public.

Although this event was really no different, the scale and brutality of the killing caused uproar. Photographs of the aftermath of the attack showed the outcome with gruesome reality, causing a demand for something to be done. That drove President Herbert

Hoover to resolve to make an example of Capone.

Although Capone was suspected of being behind the killings, he was at his mansion in Florida when they took place and supposedly had a note from his doctor confirming that he was confined to his bed. Nevertheless, it is widely believed that Capone planned the Saint Valentine's Day Massacre from his Florida mansion. McGurn was checked into a distant hotel and there was no evidence of either man's involvement, resulting in no-one ever being convicted of the crimes.

McGurn was staying at the hotel with his then girlfriend, Louise Rolfe, who claimed they had spent the whole day together in bed. Nevertheless, the police charged him with the seven murders and subsequently also charged him with crossing state lines with Rolfe, an offence at the time due to her being an unmarried woman. McGurn prevented her testifying against him by divorcing his wife and marrying Rolfe, resulting in all charges being dropped.

McGurn was later named Public Enemy Number Four at the time Capone was Number One on the list. However, he subsequently became ostracized by Capone's outfit and in 1936 was shot and killed.

The main suspects for that killing were Bugs Moran, as revenge for McGurn's part in the St. Valentine's Day Massacre, or the Chicago Outfit because he knew too much about them. McGurn was buried at Mount Carmel Cemetery in Hillside, Illinois, the same resting place as many other gangsters, including Al Capone.

The public reaction to the St. Valentine's Day Massacre added to the determination to convict Capone and was another contributory factor in his eventual downfall. He was summoned to appear before a grand jury in connection with the massacre but failed to attend, claiming he was unwell.

He was finally, in 1931, charged with contempt of court for that failure to appear and ultimately did receive a one-year jail sentence that he served after completing his time for the tax evasion charges. More crucially, since a federal court issued the contempt citation, the FBI became involved and it was their work that eventually brought about his downfall.

An estimated seven further killings took place over the next eighteen months up to 23rd October 1930 before he was found guilty of tax fraud the following year.

The Quest for Justice

Al Capone ruled by terror and murder for many years and was pursued by the police for numerous crimes without success. It is, therefore, somewhat ironic that he was eventually convicted and jailed for something as comparatively simple and harmless as tax evasion.

How Capone Evaded Justice

He avoided prosecution for a long time by a process of bribery and corruption of police and officials combined with intimidating or eliminating potential witnesses. An estimated $30 million was spent in 1927 on bribes to various people who could protect him in some way.

His own employees or associates were either fiercely loyal to him or were too fearful for their own safety to act against him. Although many people knew of his crimes, hardly any of them were prepared to say anything about them. He was also careful not to be linked with criminal acts, ensured alibis were watertight and had no properties registered in his name.

Capone dealt exclusively in cash, having no bank account in his name and apparently only ever signing one cheque (for a gambling debt), so that no transactions could be traced back to him. Nevertheless, the case against him was building slowly (the one cheque in his name being part of the evidence) and the outcome seemed increasingly inevitable.

Gaining the First Convictions

Public outcry against his activities became so great that, in March 1929, President Herbert Hoover insisted to Secretary of the Treasury Andrew Mellon that Capone must be jailed. That started the process that would eventually lead to him being convicted of tax evasion.

Prior to that, Capone's first conviction for a criminal offence came in May 1929 after he was arrested in Philadelphia for carrying a concealed weapon while on his way back from a meeting of crime bosses in Atlantic City, New Jersey. He was convicted and sentenced, within sixteen hours of his arrest, to one year in jail but was freed in March 1930 for good behavior.

One month later, Capone was named Public Enemy Number 1 by the Chicago Crime Commission when it released its first list of wanted criminals. This didn't help the reputation of a man who wanted to be viewed as a solid citizen and businessman.

The Role of Eliot Ness

Federal agent Eliot Ness has been widely credited with bringing about Capone's downfall. That's largely due to his memoirs, 'The Untouchables', which subsequently gave rise to a successful TV series and film, although it is now accepted that his role was somewhat exaggerated. The responsibility for this is largely accredited to co-author Oscar Fraley, who was the source of many of the 'facts' in the book.

Ness's small team of prohibition agents was labelled 'the Untouchables' because they supposedly could not be bribed. They raided illegal breweries and other illicit operations and were involved in Capone's indictment for prohibition violations when he was arrested after testifying to a grand jury on 27th March 1929.

Indeed, Ness's team was able to assemble a bootlegging indictment against Capone that ran to 5,000 charges. That work went to waste to some degree when the decision was later taken to prosecute on tax evasion charges instead.

Ness did succeed in angering Capone greatly by destroying or seizing millions of dollars' worth of brewing equipment, destroying thousands of gallons of alcohol, closing some large breweries and damaging his bootlegging business by exposing prohibition violations. A lot of the increased activity was undertaken after Capone murdered a friend of Ness.

Ness's Innovative Methods

Ness was at the very least innovative in his methods and beliefs. His squad cars were painted in easily recognizable colors and had two-way radios to make communication easy. He pioneered forensic science, with an emphasis on ballistic tests and soil samples, and made use of wiretapping to gather evidence.

His battle against corruption led to the setting up of teams to investigate the bribery of police officers, the forerunner of today's internal affairs divisions. And his views on alcohol and drug addiction were ahead of his time, believing that they were medical problems rather than being treated as criminal acts, as was then the prevalent thought.

Although Ness was certainly above bribery and corruption, he wasn't quite the saintly figure that was portrayed. Some of the alcohol that was impounded was given away to reporters to encourage them to cover the story and Ness himself was partial to a drink. His later years featured periods of heavy drinking after a spell as Cleveland's director of public safety and a failed attempt in 1947 to become Cleveland's mayor, before his death in 1957 at the age of 55.

Ness's death occurred shortly before 'The Untouchables' book was published Although a lot of the content was fictitious nonsense, the book told a great story and was a huge success. As were, of course, the TV series starring Robert Stack as Ness, which ran for four years from 1959, and the film starring Kevin Costner that grossed $76 million.

The Change of Tactics

One of the reasons that Capone evaded justice for so long was that different agencies were responsible for investigating his various activities and the FBI only became involved latterly. Any prohibition offences, for example, were the responsibility of the Bureau of Prohibition while the killings in the St. Valentine's Day Massacre were not classed as federal offences.

In an attempt to run Capone out of Florida, he was arrested on vagrancy charges in April 1930. In February 1931, he was tried for contempt as a result of him failing to attend a grand jury hearing after feigning illness. He was sentenced to six months in jail but was freed while he appealed the conviction.

This was the first time the FBI became involved in the pursuit of Al Capone, being asked by US Attorneys to find out if his excuse of ill-health was genuine. It proved not to be true since, despite Capone being supposedly bed-ridden at the time while suffering from bronchopneumonia, he was spotted at the race track, on holiday and was even being questioned by local prosecutors during that period. That resulted in him being cited for contempt of court and other charges followed on from there.

Preparing for the Tax Evasion Charge

A lot of the credit for Capone's later conviction for tax evasion goes to Elmer Irey, a United States Treasury Department official who was told by Secretary of the Treasury Andrew Mellon that it was the responsibility of his office to put Capone in jail. He led the Internal Revenue Service's investigative unit that built a case against him. That was only possible due to a change of law in 1927 when the Supreme Court decreed that income tax was due on illegal earnings.

This occurred during a trial against bootlegger Manley Sullivan, who was convicted of failing to file a tax return that showed the profits he made from his criminal businesses. An argument that the Fifth Amendment protected criminals from having to report illegal earnings was rejected by Justice Oliver Wendell Holmes Junior.

This cleared the way for the IRS special investigation unit to appoint Frank J Wilson, their most relentless and aggressive investigator, to investigate Capone. He was to focus on his spending as a means of proving his level of income.

Capone's income was obviously substantial since his net worth was estimated at about $30 million in 1929. Despite this, he had never filed an income tax return.

Capone had long maintained to all who would listen that he was a respectable and successful businessman. The main point he had overlooked, however, was that successful businessmen earn a good income and have to pay their taxes on that income. That was a big hole in Capone's record that the government looked to exploit.

Lavish Spending Was the Key

Capone's income was well hidden due to the lack of a bank account and no record of any assets in his name. Consequently, Wilson's team of five investigators concentrated initially on his extravagant lifestyle and uncovered purchases of Lincoln limousines, gold plated dinner services and jewel studded belt buckles. They also found evidence of the booking of luxury hotel suites, the staging of lavish parties and telephone bills amounting to $39,000.

Such levels of spending could only be possible if there was the income to match it but determining that income was little short of impossible. Although the revenue came from hundreds of sources, there was no obvious documentary evidence and no-one willing to testify against Capone. That was due to a sense of loyalty or, more likely in many cases, a fear of their lives or well-being should they dare to talk.

One who did talk was Eddie O'Hare, an operator of dog racing tracks and patent owner of the mechanical lure used in these events. He provided leads for the investigators but eventually paid with his life when he was shot to death just before Capone was released from prison.

Breakthroughs in the Investigation

The investigation ran for two years and the first real breakthrough, in 1930, was the acquisition of three bound ledgers found in a raid on one of Capone's premises. These ledgers appeared to provide evidence of income from a gambling hall although without conclusive proof that they referred to Capone.

Comparison of handwriting in the ledgers identified the author as Leslie Shumway and, having tracked him down to his Florida home; agents threatened him with a subpoena. Aware of the trouble he was in, with Capone certain to exact retribution if he were to divulge information, Shumway took protection and agreed to talk. He submitted an affidavit where he described the gambling business and admitted he took orders from Capone in relation to it.

Another important witness was Frank Reis, who was named on several cashier cheques that were assumed to be intended for Capone. After spending four days in solitary confinement, he admitted to agents that he was employed by Capone and that the cheques covered profits at his Cicero gambling hall. This evidence was later repeated in testimony to a grand jury.

In the trial that followed in 1931, the ledgers were actually inadmissible due to the statute of limitations. However, Capone's lawyers failed to make the necessary objections, although the ledgers themselves did not prove his control of the business.

Around this time, Capone's Brother Ralph was tried and convicted of tax evasion. He was sentenced to three years in prison and this prompted Al Capone to take action so the same didn't happen to him.

Capone's Crucial Mistake that Led to his Conviction

He instructed his lawyers to regularize his tax situation but, in doing so, gave the authorities the information they needed about his income. Capone was present at a meeting, in April 1930, between his tax attorney Lawrence Mattingly and investigator Frank Wilson when the stated intention was to settle his tax dues.

At that meeting, Capone nevertheless refused to admit the level of his income and grew increasingly irritated as it progressed, eventually issuing a thinly veiled threat against Wilson and his wife. Five months later, on 30th September, Capone's lawyers stated in a letter that he was willing to pay tax on income in a specific number of years.

This letter covered the six years that were in dispute. It offered that he would pay tax on Capone's income in that period, ranging from an admitted $26,000 in 1924 through to $100,000 in each of the years 1928 and 1929.

The government now had the documentary evidence it so badly needed of Capone's large amounts of income over several years. It was a grave mistake on Capone's part and resulted in him being charged in 1931 with tax evasion as well as violations of the Volstead Act (Prohibition).

The charges were backed up by other evidence gathered by Elmer Irey's team, agents having infiltrated Capone's organization at great risk to themselves. One informer was killed before he could testify but the two bookkeepers who had been employed by Capone were put under police protection before charges were brought.

The Charges against Capone

The government initially claimed Capone had a 1924 tax liability of more than $32,000, while still investigating the years 1925 to 1929. The grand jury indicted Capone for the 1924 evasion of income tax two days before the statute of limitations would have prevented this. Further counts covering the years 1925 to 1929 were added two months later.

Ultimately, the grand jury found Capone guilty of 22 counts of tax evasion in the sum of over $200,000. Additionally, he and 68 gang members were charged with 5,000 violations of the Volstead Act but the tax evasion charges were considered to have precedence over these.

These were reckoned to have the far greatest chance of success since many jurors would be likely to drink alcohol and therefore have some sympathy with Capone's activities. However, such approval was unlikely to extend to tax evasion, which was generally a detested offence.

The Plea Bargain that Failed

With doubts over the six-year statute of limitations being upheld by the Supreme Court and fears that witnesses could intimidated, US Attorney George E Q Johnson arranged a plea bargain that could see Capone being jailed for as little as two years and no more than five years.

Judge James Herbert Wilkerson, however, would have none of this and refused to allow the deal, so Capone withdrew his guilty plea. Wilkerson was keen to stress that there would be no bargaining with the Federal Government and that the parties involved in a criminal case could not determine the judgment.

How Jury Intimidation was Avoided

Instead, the trial went ahead and a vital element was Judge Wilkerson changing the jury for a fresh one at the last minute and sequestering them each night to prevent them being bribed or intimidated. The action came after the Judge learned that Capone's organization had managed to obtain a full list of all the prospective jurors and was engaged in giving out bribes and making threats to get them on his side.

That knowledge was provided by informant Eddie O'Hare to Frank Wilson, who was initially doubtful of the claims. O'Hare was able to provide a list of ten names, however, that matched those on the list of jurors that even Judge Wilkerson hadn't yet been given.

Wilson was worried that all the work done to bring Capone to trial would be wasted but his fears were allayed by Wilkerson, who was apparently unconcerned by the development. On 5th October 1931, the first day of the trial, Judge Wilkerson started proceedings by exchanging his panel of jurors for another at a trial that was due to start that day in another court.

Capone, who had smiled at the jurors as he walked into court with his bodyguards, was visibly taken aback by this turn of events. The 23 charges of tax evasion against him were then outlined in front of the twelve jurors — all men, since female jurors were not allowed in Illinois until 1939.

The Evidence Against Capone

As various witnesses were called, the evidence against Capone slowly mounted. Tax collector Charles W Arndt affirmed that Capone had not filed any tax returns for the years 1924 to 1929 while Cicero citizen Chester Bragg testified that Capone had clearly stated that he was the owner of the Hawthorne Smoke Shop, a Cicero gambling hall.

That occurred during a citizens' raid on the place and the Reverend Henry Hoover, who led the raid, recalled that Capone had threatened the participants. Some of the most damning evidence came from Leslie Shumway, who had been the cashier at the Hawthorne Smoke Shop. He estimated that profits of over $550,000 accrued during the two years he worked there but was reluctant to identify Capone as the owner, although he did confirm he was in charge of the business.

Crucial to the case was Judge Wilkerson allowing the letter from Capone's lawyers to be admitted into evidence. He over-ruled an objection that, in effect, a lawyer could not make a confession on behalf of his client. This followed agent Frank Wilson's description of Lawrence Mattingly delivering the letter and stating that Capone was willing to pay the tax liability arising from the income shown on it.

Lengthy evidence of Capone's spending was presented by US Attorney Johnson and he emphasized the hypocrisy of someone who, while claiming to be a man of the people, spent obscene amounts of money on himself and gave relatively little to others. More crucially, the high levels of spending were evidence of the income that Capone achieved but did not declare to the tax authorities.

Evidence of Capone's lavish spending came from several witnesses. One of these was Parker Henderson Junior, who had acted as Capone's real estate representative. He recalled that he'd shown Capone several properties in Florida, resulting in him buying the mansion on Palm Island. Another witness testified to seeing large amounts of cash at the property.

Similarly, a clerk at the Metropole Hotel in Chicago told how Capone held lavish parties there and booked the most expensive suites. All of this was paid for in cash, in large denomination bills.

Frank Reis, cashier at the Hawthorne Smoke Shop in 1927, reckoned the profits there that year were about $150,000. This money was used to purchase a large number of cashier's cheques, at least one of which bore Al Capone's signature.

Failure of the Defence Case

Once the prosecution had presented its evidence, the defense took only one day to make its case and did not do a very good job. Having failed to object to the ledgers being brought into evidence due to the statute of limitations, it then presented a mistaken defense based on gambling losses.

It depicted Capone as a gambling addict who had lost the money his business had earned. Since gambling losses could only be offset against winnings, however, this didn't excuse him from paying tax on his business income.

The defense case that Capone had lost $327,000 over six years and this matched his taxable income was totally spurious. In summing up, defense attorney Albert Fink denied there was sufficient evidence of Capone's gross income and accused the government of being determined to convict him at all costs. Whilst pleading that the jury should not convict Capone just because he was a bad person, he also tried to depict his good side and said he was not a tax cheat.

In his summing up, prosecutor Jacob Grossman stressed that Capone's lavish spending was obvious evidence of a very large income and that the letter submitted by lawyer Mattingly proved that Capone knew he had committed tax evasion. US Attorney George Jackson claimed the case would establish whether someone could conduct his affairs in such a way that he was above the law.

The Verdict that Ended Capone's Criminal Career

On 17th October 1931, after deliberating for only nine hours, the jury found Al Capone guilty of tax evasion on several counts. Although he was acquitted on most counts and found guilty of only five, these were enough for the judge to hand down a sentence that was far above the normal level for this type of offence.

He was sentenced to eleven years in jail and ordered to pay court costs of $30,000 and $50,000 in fines as well as the $215,000 plus interest he owed in back taxes. This was the harshest sentence ever imposed for tax fraud, one that visibly shocked Capone and his lawyers.

To appeal the conviction, Capone appointed a Washington-based law firm that was expert in tax law. They filed a writ of habeas corpus, stating that the charges were outside the time limit for prosecution due to the Supreme Court having ruled that tax evasion was not classed as fraud. The judge overruled the appeal by deducting the time Capone had spent in Miami from the length of time since the offences.

Effect of the Conviction

That was the end of Capone's criminal career. His role within organized crime in Chicago ceased immediately although the organization he had previously headed simply carried on under new leadership. A succession of bosses followed him, chiefly Frank Nitti, Paul Ricca, Tony Accardo and

Sam Giancana from amongst his previous followers.

The level of violence decreased, however, and Capone's successors adopted a lower profile than he had done. With the end of Prohibition in 1933, the extent of the criminal activities naturally diminished. Nevertheless, the levels of gambling, prostitution and various other illegal activities continued pretty much as before.

One perhaps surprising consequence of Capone's conviction was that back tax receipts went up, both from criminals and law-abiding citizens. That year, the value of unpaid tax filings paid doubled to over $1 million compared to the previous year.

Final Days

In May 1932, at the age of 33 and weighing almost 18 stones, Capone arrived at Atlanta US Penitentiary. A medical examination there revealed that the use of cocaine had perforated his septum and he was suffering from withdrawal symptoms as a result of his addiction. He was also diagnosed as having syphilis and gonorrhoea, the results of his time working in brothels, and which would lead to further deterioration in his health.

His mental health was already showing signs of failing and he was seen as a weak personality who could not deal with bullying. He required the protection of cellmate Red Rudinsky, formerly a minor associate of Capone's gang, which drew accusations of special treatment.

This belief of favoritism was borne out by the conditions under which he lived. Despite his delicate mental state, he was able to use his influence to procure special privileges, furnishings and other items that made his life easier.

His cell had a carpet, personal bedding and other expensive furnishings. There was also a radio and Capone and various inmates and guards would converse and listen to favorite programs. Visitors were plentiful, with friends and family members maintaining a residence in a nearby hotel.

The Transfer to Alcatraz

Partly because of this, and also to provide publicity for the newly opened Alcatraz Federal Penitentiary in San Francisco Bay, Capone was moved there in June 1936. Alcatraz was a maximum security prison intended for violent inmates or those with disciplinary issues. Capone did not fall into those categories so the gaining of publicity for the new facility seemed the most logical reason for moving him there.

Soon after arriving at Alcatraz, Capone was stabbed and slightly wounded by another inmate. The assailant was James 'Tex' Lucas, a 22-year old Texan who was serving thirty years in federal prison for auto theft and bank robbery.

He turned out to be a trouble-maker after transferring to Alcatraz from Leavenworth, since he was later involved in a work strike followed by a violent escape attempt in which a prison officer was killed. Lucas received a life sentence for that and a spell in solitary confinement.

The attack on Capone, on 23rd June 1936, was, he alleged, in response to a threat to kill Lucas. He attacked Capone in the shower room, striking him with one half of a pair of scissors and inflicting superficial cuts to his chest and hands. For the offence, Lucas lost his accumulated time for good behavior, a total of 3,600 days.

During his time in Alcatraz, Capone remained a celebrity. There were constant questions from the press regarding his well-being, activities and anything else about him. Even many years after his death, the cell he occupied is one of the main visitor attractions on 'the Rock'.

Capone's syphilis caused the onset of dementia and eroded his mental capacity. The doctors tried to eradicate the syphilis with malaria injections, hoping the induced fever would clear it.

The treatment almost killed Capone and he spent the last twelve months at Alcatraz in the prison hospital in a confused state. On 6th January 1939, he was released and transferred to the Federal Correctional Institution at Terminal Island near Los

Angeles, to serve a twelve-month sentence for the contempt of court conviction.

Release from Prison and Hospital Treatment

Capone was paroled on 16th November 1939 and referred to John Hopkins Hospital in Baltimore for treatment of syphilis-related illnesses. Admission was refused because of who he was and instead he was admitted to the Union Memorial Hospital. There he became one of the first civilian patients to be administered penicillin as treatment for his syphilis, although by now the condition was far too advanced for it to have much effect.

After several weeks of in-patient and out-patient treatment, Capone left Baltimore on 20th March 1940, donating two Japanese weeping cherry trees to the hospital as thanks for the care he had received. He returned to his mansion on Palm Island for the remaining years of his life, passing the time playing cards and fishing. Test conducted in 1946 by his physician and a psychiatrist concluded that he had the mental capacity of a twelve-year old child.

Capone spent his final days being cared for by his wife and brothers. Most of his time was spent wearing pajamas and having conversations with enemies and colleagues who had died years before, some of them on his orders.

He was reportedly paid by the Outfit a salary of $600 a week, which was barely enough to support his family, pay his staff and maintain the property. Wife Mae kept him in isolation during his last years, knowing any loose public statements about his old organization could well cost him his life while violent outburst brought on by his condition would lose him his freedom.

Illness and Death

Capone suffered a stroke on 21st January 1947. Although he began to recover, he then contracted pneumonia and, on 22nd January, suffered a cardiac arrest.

He died three days later at the age of 48 with his family around him and his physician asked if an autopsy could be conducted on his brain and body for the purposes of medical research. This was refused by the family and the body went to the Philbrick

Funeral Home in Miami Beach where it was placed in a $2,000 massive bronze casket.

The body was available for viewing by permitted guests only although two funeral home employees apparently took surreptitious photographs of Al Capone lying in his open coffin. Huge quantities of flowers arrived and the funeral service was held the following Wednesday at St. Patrick's Roman Catholic Church.

Final Resting Place

Capone was buried at Mount Olivet Cemetery in Chicago close to his father and one brother. Three years afterwards, to counter the constant attention and the vandalism of the gravestone, all the family remains were removed to Mount Carmel

Cemetery in Hillside, Illinois. The original monument was left in place in Mount Olivet Cemetery in an unsuccessful attempt to prevent visitors learning of the new location of the remains.

In a strange twist of fate, Capone died only five days after Andrew John Volstead at the age of 86. Volstead was a member of the United States House of Representatives who, while serving as chairman of the House Judiciary Committee, co-authored the National Prohibition Act of 1916 that bears his name. The act enabled the enforcement of Prohibition, with Capone's subsequent criminal career partly based on the evasion of that legislation.

Mae continued to live in the Palm Island mansion for another five years until she was forced to sell it. She died in 1986, aged 89, but not before she had destroyed all her diaries and private papers relating to Al Capone.

The Capone Legacy

Despite Capone's violent career and the brutality of his past, there is an on-going fascination with his life. Many fictitious characters have been modelled on him and the term 'mobster' or 'gangster' invariably conjures up an image of Al Capone.

There have been plenty of books and articles covering his life and some of these have been made into films. The most well-known of these is Eliot Ness's biography 'The Untouchables', which subsequently became a successful TV series and then a major film. As in many cases, however, the facts weren't always faithfully recorded and the roles of individuals are sometimes exaggerated.

In real life, Capone's influence was enough to change the law in order to deal with him. The 1927 Supreme Court ruling that income tax was due on criminal earnings was intended to help the authorities trap criminals and was instrumental in Capone's eventual downfall.

The End of Prohibition

Later on, the end of the Prohibition era in 1933 was brought about because many Americans enjoyed going to a speakeasy and having a drink. Additionally, it was obvious that Prohibition was actually encouraging criminal activity and many gangsters were getting rich through their bootlegging activities.

So maybe Al Capone's greatest legacy is, ironically, that through violence and brutality, he changed the laws of America. In order to stop him and his peers, activities that he'd undertaken illegally were made legal.

Although there are the contrasting images that Capone leaves behind — on the one hand a do-gooder who helped the poor and on the other a mobster who thought nothing of torturing and killing his opponents — many of his relatives have responded to the bad side. Some have changed their names and moved away from Chicago while others have refused to talk about him or have done so only under the cover of anonymity.

Despite his notoriety as a mobster, one of the biggest ironies of all is that Capone spent longer in jail than he did as a leading criminal. His reign as a crime boss ended after six years at the age of 33. He was then to spend the next seven years six months and fifteen days in prison before his eventual release on parole.

Ongoing Fascination with Capone

The fascination with Capone appears to show little sign of slackening, even seventy years after his death. A recent auction in June 2017 saw a diamond studded platinum pocket watch that belonged to him sold for $84,375.

The triangular watch, on a fourteen carat white gold chain, features 23 diamonds in the shape of his initials, surrounded by a further 26 diamonds and another 72 diamonds on the watch face. Also sold at the auction, for $18,750, was a musical composition — 'Humanesque' — written by Capone in pencil while imprisoned in Alcatraz.

In September 2016, a letter from Capone sold for $62,500 at an auction in Massachusetts. Written to his son from his cell in Alcatraz, the letter, according to experts, showed Capone's softer side.

The Chicago History Museum's website still gets 50,000 hits a month on pages about Capone while visitors to Chicago still drive past his old home and visit his grave site, even though the body is no longer there.

However, the city has made little effort to publicize or preserve the sites associated with Capone, not wishing to draw attention to its violent past.

Capone's Palm Island estate sold for $7.4 million in 2014. It is now available for hire to use for private functions or events, so the fascination with Capone still endures.

Made in the USA
Monee, IL
05 December 2020